THE CAPTAIN'S
TOWER

for Bob Dylan
on his seventieth birthday
May 24th 2011

THE CAPTAIN'S TOWER

Seventy Poets Celebrate Bob Dylan
at Seventy

Foreword by Ronnie Wood

Edited by
Phil Bowen
Damian Furniss
David Woolley

Seren is the book imprint of
Poetry Wales Press Ltd,
57 Nolton Street, Bridgend, Wales, CF31 3AE

Explore thirty years of fine writing at
www.serenbooks.com

For readings: thecaptainstower@gmail.com

First published 2011

ISBN: 978-1-85411-560-7

A CIP record for this title is available from the British Library.

The publisher acknowledges the financial assistance of the Welsh Books
Council.

Printed by Bell & Bain Ltd, Glasgow

Author and editorial fees, and royalties from the sales of *The Captain's Tower*
will be paid to CRISIS, a registered charity numbers E&W1082947, SC040094

www.crisis.org.uk is the national charity for single homeless people, support-
ed by Bob Dylan through the release of his *Christmas in the Heart* album.

Mixed Sources
Product group from well-managed
forests and other controlled sources
www.fsc.org Cert no. TT-COC-002769
© 1996 Forest Stewardship Council

FSC

CONTENTS

FOREWORD

I always enjoy getting together with Bob. It doesn't happen often, but good things come out of it. Bob and I have a kind of unwritten rule: when we're in the studio together, we can leave a lot unsaid because, being fellow Geminis, we understand what's coming next, don't have to discuss it. So we draw a lot together and strum and talk through the guitar.

Bob is a man who adapts and blends, who searches and leads at the same time, who asks questions, and answers them at once. He cracks a crime, then investigates. His scope in everyday living is talking through poetry – sending poignant messages through his voice, guitar, piano and punctuating sometimes with pencil and brush, heart and pen.

And his work touches a lot of people, speaks to musicians, novelists, painters and, to judge from *The Captain's Tower*, poets. Here are many poets, from Ginsberg, Ferlinghetti and McClure who have worked and toured with Dylan for decades, to young twentysomethings who recognise his enduring genius. Poets of all schools, writing in all styles, from America, Britain, Ireland, Australia, New Zealand. Dylan has spoken to them, provoked, inspired, moved them; now they speak back to him.

Ronnie Wood

EDITORIAL

'...Ezra Pound and T.S. Eliot
fighting in the captain's tower...'
Bob Dylan, 'Desolation Row'

'I don't call myself a poet because I don't like the word. I call myself a trapeze artist.' We don't call Bob Dylan a poet either, we call him a songwriter. He has written poems – spontaneous compositions in the style of the Beats – and the lucid prose of his memoir *Chronicles* has poetic qualities, but he works language to fit music. From what we know of his changing approaches to composition, his lyrics flow with or from that music, don't precede it; we judge them on those terms.

The folk tradition he belongs to values immortality over originality, knows a song is born of a man and a mountain of men. His songs parody, quote, ask questions of and respond to their predecessors; as he has had to learn the craft he once practised unconsciously, he's felt free to raid other literary sources where they suit his purposes. Poem, story and song were once all one, but as literary culture emerged with the printing press, the practice of poetry and song-writing diverged. Poets respond to Bob Dylan like no other musician because he takes us back to our common ancestry.

Though written for the voice, poems survive on the page, are framed by the space they are set in; songs prosper in performance, are transmitted through their recordings. Bob Dylan is seventy, and he's spent fifty of those years behind a microphone. No doubt musicians will celebrate the occasion in their own way, but this anthology retells the tale familiar to many biographies as only poets can, following his creative journey through our lives and his, but also reflecting the polyphony of poetries that have echoed from the captain's tower in his lifetime.

Bob Dylan donated all the royalties from his 2009 album *Christmas in the Heart* to Crisis, the national charity for single homeless people, and our contributors have done likewise to mark the birthday of the patron of hobos and maker of the soundtrack to our lives. We thank all the writers who responded to our call, and in so many different ways, but most of all we thank him. Many happy returns!

Damian Furniss

HAPPY SEVENTIETH BIRTHDAY BLUES

I'm staring into seventy, staring at the old bad news,
Yeah, staring into seventy, staring at the rank bad news.
I'm getting slowly smashed, but it's not the getting smashed
                                        you'd choose.

It's a wall without a garden, shining on the other side,
A wall without a pardon, smiling on the other side –
Just ask any angel who ever crossed that divide.

I heard the devil singing, he was singing to me long ago.
He sang me through the '60s, he sang to me years ago –
Sang *Man, if you're a woman, you just have to grow and grow.*

I'm a long-born woman, and it's the shortest straw.
I'm a long-born woman, smoking my cheroot of straw.
But I'm no damned angel, I was born to be a whole lot more.

I'm looking at the wall. Are you telling me it's a gate?
I'm looking at a wall, yeah, he's telling me it's the gate.
You can find it if you're blind, baby-blue, it's not too late

We're only ever twenty, we're only ever at the start.
We're only ever peddling that iconic parabolic start,
And there's no wall, baby, it's the shadow of an empty heart.

Go cruising into seventy, seventy's a broad high-way;
Cruise along at seventy, along that broad high-way –
You'll soon be doing eighty, if the angels get out the way.

Carol Rumens

EIDOLON

Down in fame's flood, down an alley, down
wind of now, elegant in self-denial,
an Iron Range wraith junking cue cards, an ideal,
an idol before which the Zeitgeist kneeled.

Dylan, named for a poet named from an old
tale of the child who crawled to the sea, this land
is yours: the black plain the needle
ploughs from lip to label; be all, end all.

Roddy Lumsden

MINNESOTA HARMONICA MAN

Open-cast mining country, a hole so vast
the diggers looked as tippable as toys
if you stood on the rim and gazed across it;
iron for world wars, iron for Korea,

but thinning. Scraggly grass and mud, the light
grey as age in the early days of autumn,
when first frost prickled and the mountains shook
in the wind that seemed to be always blowing,

blowing and sucking. Shrunken forests,
spruce and fir, pines, moccasin country,
a map freckled with water, bogs absorbing
the blue-green needles of the tamarack.

The freight-train whistles blew and sucked. Their wail
hung in the steady and insistent gusts
like a come-hither fading with the dusk.
Night was indoors, the sound of parents' friends.

All you could be was family or elsewhere.
A boy lounged on the main drag.
He was pretending he was James Dean,
he was pretending he was Baudelaire.

Small wonder, then, if home became a spotlight,
as, blowing and sucking, you count the changes,
wearing a hood like a cowl to shut
out the sound of the everlasting wind

that blows from childhood, blows to suck you back.
There's no solace or ease now for the soul
that kicked the mine-dust from its heels. Sometimes
the one comfort is never standing still.

Lachlan MacKinnon

BOB AND BUDDY AT THE ARMORY

A twitchy kid with vertical
hair taps a single boot heel

as the Winter Dance Party
tries to thaw the chilly Duluth Armory.

Outside, a band of snow
moves south-eastwards through

Minnesota
and North Dakota.

The kid with the School Yearbook quiff
drums a Little Richard riff

on his metallic folding chair,
squints at Frankie Sardo the square,

when suddenly, there's Buddy walking on,
fifteen feet from Robert Allen Zimmerman.

Their eyes connect for a second
before the cavernous sound

of Buddy strumming his electric guitar,
singing a song about winter

coming on,
how he feels like travelling on.

Terry Kelly

IMAGES FROM PETER BLAKE AND CLAES OLDENBURG (1962) / THE MANDRAX VARIATIONS

Fingers drum on monochrome steering-wheel
(Dada dit, Dada dit)
with impatience stolen from James Dean,
impatient for the lights to change,
impatient for the lights to swell out,
engulf the air, engulf the supermarkets
where people queue in silent sepia tints,
engulf the drabness of streets,
the emptiness of sky.
Fingers drum on monochrome steering-wheel
(Dada dit, Dada dit)
thinking of half-completed erotic collages
that no-one will exhibit,
thinking of multi-coloured butterflies
leaving muddy foot-marks across
a severed retina,
thinking of carved wooden grasshoppers
crawling out of amphetamine midnight walls.
Waiting for the lights to change.
Waiting for the world to change.
Fingers drum on monochrome steering-wheel
(Dada dit, Dada dit)
open-top American car, wind-tangled hair,
dumb insolence practised from early Presley movies,
in angular reflecting American wing-mirror,
like a segment of a picture he's yet to create
overlaid with Munroe, Bikini Atoll and CND symbols,
like a jerky sporadic target
on a blaring fairground silkscreen,
like a cut-out on a cereal packet
of Kennedy or Gargarin,
like the photograph of a pop star
in a locket on a schoolgirl's chain

DADA DIT, DADA DIT, RED AMBER GREEN, RED
AMBER GREEN,

DADADIT, DADADIT, REDAMBERGREEN,
REDAMBERGREEN,
DADADIT.

It is 1962.
Beatles in a Hamburg cellar.
Dylan in a Greenwich Village Coffee House.
I am 15.

Andrew Darlington

HOW DYLAN BECAME
SOMEONE ELSE

In the days when Dylan meant Thomas, we were a clique
of duffle-coated misfits out of grammar school.
We used to crash in my downstairs flat
pretending it was a beatnik pad;
listened to Charlie Parker and Miles Davis,
duly despising Beatlemania.
We seldom ventured on the road –
read Kerouac instead; thought we should smoke
something, chose Gaullois (hash on the streets those days
was scarce – at least in Bridgwater.)

One day Hotdog came round. *Hey, man* he said *listen to*
                                                    this.
We listened –
            the frail white youth on the record sleeve;
the raw shock of the voice, like a freight of coal
dragged through the delicate portal of a flower.

Like Shelley had swallowed America.

One man and his guitar – this was something new.
It matched our stance of existential bravado.
We got stoned on that first eponymous LP
and, after that, *Freewheelin'*.

With *The Times They Are A-Changin'*, things went wrong.
A diverted stampede, the Beatle-howling girls
all changed direction. We were appalled:
this wasn't supposed to happen.
We gave up on him as soon as he went electric;
solemnly told each other he'd *sold out*.

Scattered now and having sold out ourselves,
we read of the comeback concert – also sold out,
but to a somewhat younger set than ours.
These are the ones who adopted our orphaned hobo,
the poet who failed to die young.
We glance at the review, feeling perhaps
a touch of wistful pride, remembering
how we discovered him first.

Anthony Watts

NEAR CRASTER

watching the Great Whin Sill
play its final hand;
decks stacked crooked in the long-ago
sliding in a shuffle to the sea,
the black cuts splitting
blue into churning jism

tides galumping in the rock kern,
Dylan chords muttering in my skull
kernhow your weary tune kernhow
in echoes of Breton Jacquerie

all rhythms begin here
strumming time with the ocean
    off-shore the eiders ride it out;
    fighter-jets swing in
    low, silent, over the waves
nu scylun hergan hefaenricaes Uard

Gordon Wardman

A STRANGER LEANING

I belong to everything and nothing... I would say
I am with all rebels everywhere all the time as
against all people who are satisfied
— Carl Sandburg

Who had walked and written, looking not unlike
Norman Bates but as an angel,
whiter-than-paper hair, and the lean
face as if after some harrowing toil –
was found but right at the end of his walking,
after the settling of his work on the world, dark
rain on the dry farms of North Carolina,
the hobo, the poet, the goat farmer,
was creasing his brow at the passing Dylan:
why was this skinny boy coming to meet him?
He puzzled and smiled, at home in the distance,
behind his white head Sugarloaf Mountain:

'You look like you are ready for anything.
I'd like to ask you 'bout forty good questions!'
he growled but he had no idea who this was,
but knew what he did, in ways he would know:
the lost blue eyes and the trails on a palm
(*the peace of great prairies be for you.*)
Dust and sunlight. Dust and sun.
                                                  When
clouds come up over Big Glassy Mountain,
troubling the old and the young together,
bless, whoever, and bless, however,
and bless, whatever. Rain on the dust,
freshen the wrinkled brow when the blue Ford
transit is going, with a stranger leaning,
ragged and sleepy, into the weather.

Glyn Maxwell

GIRL FROM THE NORTH

Transported, three thousand miles away
from home, I'm driving into New York Town,

down 5th in my blue VW – Kombi '61 – heading
for the Village, West 4th # 161, top floor,

I'll park right outside his door. Ahead, stretch
stop-lights, sychronised: *drive, don't drive.*

By the time I reach West 4th there's no place
to wait outside his door, so I drive some more,

down Macdougal, past the Wha – I've
brought my guitar. On my tenth go-round

I skid on Bleecker, forced to make a right
up Jones, tyres sliding over ice-hard

snow. Gone midnight. Ten below. *Coldest
winter in nineteen years*, the radio says,

and I thank my stars when the wheels come to rest –
nearest I'm gonna get. Wondering what's going on

in 161, I strum a few chords – *follow me down* –
wrap my old greatcoat around, so warm, so warm.

Waking early, half chilled to death, it takes
the plectrum to scrape my breath, frozen

to the windows while I slept. That's when
I see a guy with his girl, walking right down

the middle of the road, hunched inside a summer
suede jerkin, while she's wrapped snug in her loden coat,

so warm, so warm; rests her head on his shoulder – to me
he seems older – hair falling down her back as they

walk, just walk, like nobody's watching, he
doesn't look up when the man with the camera calls:

Hey, Bobby, let's do that one more time. No coat –
he could freeze to the bone, I'll give him mine,

but he keeps on walking as snow turns to slush
under his black boots and his breath rises

like smoke on the air; I see it form into words
and chords I've learned by heart, and I'm back,

out on the fire escape taking one more drag, last
fag on my morning break, before I head down

to the shop floor. Saturday girl in a Bolton store,
I like to live in the frame, freewheel every car.

Pamela Johnson

SUCK YOUR GLASSES

the journalist said
to Dylan at the press show,
just twenty-three in '64.
I think he wanted him
to look English.

Chinese lantern of his jaws,
palest white, eyes
succour flames,
at ease, at first,
then biting the cynical.

Confused, he hands the shades
to the journalist to demonstrate.
Impatient with the kid
he says *Look, like this*
and starts to suck
on the left ear-hook

as the room watches

Chris McCabe

HARD RAIN

After I heard *It's a Hard Rain's A-Gonna Fall*
played softly by an accordion quartet
through the ceiling speakers at the Springdale Shopping
Mall,
I understood: there's nothing
we can't pluck the stinger from,

nothing we can't turn into a soft-drink flavor or a t-shirt.
Even serenity can become something horrible
if you make a commercial about it
using smiling, white-haired people

quoting Thoreau to sell retirement homes
in the Everglades, where the swamp has been
drained and bulldozed into a nineteen-hole golf course
with electrified alligator barriers.

'You can't keep beating yourself up, Billy,'
I heard the therapist say on television
                    to the teenage murderer,
'about all these people you killed –
You just have to be the best person you can be,
                    one day at a time –'

And everybody in the audience claps and weeps a little,
because the level of deep feeling has been touched,
and they want to believe that
the power of Forgiveness is greater
than the power of Consequence, or History.

Dear Abby:
My father is a businessman who travels.
Each time he returns from one of his trips,
his shoes and trousers
    are covered with blood –
but he never forgets to bring me a nice present.
Should I say something?
                    Signed, America.

I used to think I was not part of this,
that I could mind my own business and get along,

but that was just another song
that has been taught to me since birth –

whose words I was humming under my breath,
as I was walking through the Springdale Mall.

Tony Hoagland

BOB DYLAN AND THE
BLUE ANGEL

What benign stroke of fate took Bob Dylan
to the Blue Angel Club after a gig at the Liverpool Empire
in 1965 remains a mystery. But there he was, seemingly alone,
all tousled up and shy, with Cilla goofing at the bar,
and Freddie Starr on stage downstairs.

Alan 'The man who gave the Beatles away' Williams
introduced us. 'He's a poet too.' So we talked poets and poetry,
music and lyrics, and soon we'd talked our way out of the club,
away from the noise and the crowd
and into the history of rock 'n' roll.

At the intersection of Bold Street and Hardman Street
he stopped. 'I'm at the crossroads, Rog,' he said.
'I can see that Bob,' I said. 'No, I mean my career,
I don't know which way to turn.' 'Seems clear to me mate,
let's have a coffee and I'll put you straight.'

So over cappuccino in the Picasso I laid it all out.
Dump the acoustic. Forget the folksy stuff and go electric.
Get yourself a band. I remember the look on his face.
Sort of relief. The tension in the trademark
hunched shoulders seemed to melt away.

Hit the booze, make friends with cocaine
to get that druggy feel. Divorce your wife, the pain will pay off
in hard-won lyrics. His eyes closed, the bottom lip trembled,
Poet to poet, you asked for my advice.
I'm not here to give you an easy ride.

Ten years from now you'll be an icon. Sounds nice
but trust me, go against the flow. Dismantle the status.
Reinvent yourself. Embrace the faith of your fathers
then give Christianity a go. With nothing to lose
make albums that serve to confound and confuse.

Then consolidate. A Lifetime Achievement Award,
and then perhaps an Oscar. By the time you're sixty...
He smiled, 'Hold on there, boy we ain't never
gonna grow old.' 'You're right, Bob.' We laughed
and made our way back to his hotel.

On the moonlit steps of the Adelphi
we exchanged phone numbers and addresses.
Suddenly he looked young and vulnerable.
Mumbling his thanks he hurried towards the entrance.
'Don't forget to write,' I called. But he never did. Never did.

Roger McGough

KILLING TIME #2

Time in the brain cells sweating like a nail bomb,
trouble with the heartbeat spitting like a Sten gun,
      cut to the chase,
      pick up the pace;
no such thing as a walkabout fun-run,
      shoot yourself a glance in the chrome in the day-room
don't hang about, you're running out of space, son.

Red light, stop sign, belly full of road rage,
ticket from the fuzz if you dawdle in the slow lane,
      pull up your socks,
      get out of the blocks;
twelve-hour day-shift grafting at the coal face,
      turning up the gas brings blood to the boat race,
strike with the iron or you're sleeping in the stone age.

Don't dilly dally or the trail goes cold, sir,
don't hold back till you're mouldy old dough, sir,
      sprint for the line,
      turn on a dime;
sit tight, hang fire, I'm putting you on hold, sir,
      too late, snail pace, already sold, sir,
blame it on the kids but it's you getting old, sir.

Short cut, fast track, trolley dash at Kwik Save,
four minute warning, boil yourself an egg, babe,
      crack the whip,
      shoot from the hip;
close shave, tear arse, riding on a knife blade,
      twenny-four-seven in the brain-drain rat race,
finger on the pulse but you'd better watch your heart rate.

Cheap thrills, speed kills, pop yourself a pill, mate,
thumb a free ride on amphetamine sulphate,
　　　run with the pack,
　　　don't look back;
pedal to the floor when you're burning up the home
straight,
　　　her indoors doesn't want you getting home late,
love's in the freezer and your dinner's in the dog-grate.

Ten to the dozen to the grave from the carry-cot,
bolt like a thoroughbred, talk like a chatterbox,
　　　oil the wheels,
　　　pick up your heels;
ginseng tea turns out to be tommyrot,
　　　reach for the future with a hand full of liver-spots,
fuse-wire burns in the barrel of a body-clock.

Cut yourself in half doing life at the sharp end,
meet your own self coming back around the U-bend,
　　　get with the beat,
　　　turn up the heat;
sink like a stone by going off the deep end,
　　　fifty quid an hour for a top-flight shrink, said
start killing time, it's later than you think, friend.

Simon Armitage

AISLE SIXTEEN (REVISITED)

Well, Big Frank the banker was pinstriped and neat
coked up to his eyeballs and chewing his cheek
when dreaming of methods to catch out the meek
an underling entered and started to speak:
Please sir, I need help our investors are starting to scream.
The big man just smiled and replied quite serene:
Take all toxic assets to Aisle Sixteen.

The slick perma-tanned arch-svengali of pop
was telling a crowd how he climbed to the top
he boasted of hits and he laughed off the flops
the slavering audience gave him his props.
Please tell us, they cried, *how you find all these synthetic teens?*
Much later he laughed in his black limousine
I find them, he whispered, *on Aisle Sixteen.*

Well, Kelvin the Killjoy stirred hatred for cash
and most of the nation woke up to his trash
each morning's invective a post-modern mash
of homos and foreigners ripe for a bash.
With underlined adjectives Kelvin would empty his spleen
and crass little Englanders drank it like cream.
The name of this column was Aisle Sixteen.

In tenement Krakow the rumours were rife
a Polish professor petitioned his wife:
The good strength of sterling could mean a new life
Lord praise the EU, we can live where we like.
But now he serves lager to kids wearing Armani jeans
and she receives two pounds an hour to clean
the mock Tudor mansions on Aisle Sixteen.

The young politician – no stranger to spin
a neat line in sound bites and translucent skin
he turned to the press with an odious grin
and said: *my dear people where do I begin?*
We've done all we can, took advice from a specialist team.
Our policy has been approved by the Queen –
we're outsourcing Britain to Aisle Sixteen.

Luke Wright

ROLLING A CIGARETTE WITH DYLAN

I love the way the paper feels
between my fingers like the wing a child might pull
off the dead body of a wasp. Rain outside
because oh children
don't we get sad. I like to watch the tobacco fall like dark
brown snow around my feet and then roll
the thing tighter than a nurse
tucking in your bed before you get to lie down in it and die.
The first drag pulling up like a muscle car
in the street of your mouth, the first exhale exploding into
the air
like Dylan's electric set at the Royal Albert Hall –
that great fuck you
sent out into the dark crowd, that beautiful I love you only
now I love you in a different way, a hard
and wild way. And when the crowd turned like a drunk on
his wife
the wife set his bed on fire. I like that fire. I like the match
exploding to life between my fingers
and that I have the power to blow it out, the power to strike
another one.

Matthew Dickman

A POSTCARD OF A HANGING

for Padraig Rooney

I sent you a postcard of a hanging,
the first one I attended, not thinking
I'd like it, or even stand it, as you
must have loathed my postcard too
till you realised it must be a trick,
a decadent, oriental gimmick
to put liberals off their breakfast
of an egg, toast, jam and the rest.

I imagine your laughs then, the card
propped against the milk, as you read
again how I thrived in the East –
every meal a ginger and chilli feast;
the girls; the boys…; how vibrant
the hours and how little I spent.
And you believed it, you knew
that all my varied antics were true.

And you turned to the picture again,
a colour print – a gallows, two men,
one hooded, one holding a noose
of whitest rope, for the moment loose,
and low in the foreground, a crowd
of men mainly, silently loud,
all eastern, except for two or three –
one of whom, if you look closely, is me.

Matthew Sweeney

TWO STORIES

The first –
I'm walking home along the Knavesmire.
Down by the racing posts
teenagers are drinking, laughing.
(Sometimes, in the evening, I call from the roadside rail
and voices cry back.)

I sit down on the grass,
pull the red wine from my bag
and ask for an opener.

'Are you a cop?'
'No. A teacher.'
'We've seen you.'
'Where?'
'In the cafe, with your girlfriend.
You're really a teacher? Coolest
teacher we ever saw.'
I go round, shake their hands.

'This is Julie,' (she's about sixteen)
'we used to go out,' says my guide.
'You left this man, Julie? What were you thinking?'

They put on a little display –
she sits across his chest. They bicker.

I take to drinking, and as usual this comes out:
'Seven songs in, before the final song,
a shout –

he strums the opening chords
to "Like a Rolling Stone"...'

'Scarper!' Everyone is running,
running from the torchlight which comes towards me.

'Stop!'
It is a woman's voice. I don't want to disobey,
complicate things, so I walk towards her.
She is twenty-five, pretty, and with a boy of about eight.

'What are you doing here?'
'I was walking home when I heard shouting,
and then I saw your light.'

We walk up to the kissing gate
and she radios in –
'I've caught two of them.'
I see my girlfriend walking home from her shift.

'What am I being held on?'
'I didn't say I *was* holding you –
supplying alcohol to minors, if anything.'
'It's just I've got to clean the flat
before my girlfriend gets home.'

At the all-night garage,
ahead of me in the queue a week later,
my guide is buying *Haagen Dazs*.
I slip away.

Two or three weeks pass. Some teenagers,
six or so, are filling the pavement.
I keep my head down.
Over my shoulder: '*Judas*!'

*

The second –
a Thai girl writes me: Bob Dylan?
When I hear him, I want to *cook*.

Matt Bryden

BACKBAY

circa 1966

It was that second floor apartment,
corner of Commonwealth & Mass. Ave.
The cops burst in, guns drawn.
They leapt in through doorways,
landing with legs spread, gun barrels
and eyes synchronized, scanning the rooms.
But it was the wrong place, a bum steer.
Even so, Fortin and whatever-his-name-was
refused to stop or acknowledge them.
The game was too close to call.
They had shoved the furniture aside,
taken the pictures off the wall
– converted the living room
into a handball court.
In shorts, sneakers, head-bands,
sweating like mad, they played
with a jaw-clenching intensity
that drew the cops over.
One looked at me, jutted his chin,
jerked his thumb toward the game.
I answered him with a shrug, showed him
my hands, palm up, explanationless.
They holstered their pistols and watched
as serves were met with a dive, a leap,
a floor-slamming lunge that made
the tone arm bounce across 'Rainy Day Women'.
It was ferocious, electrifying.
Swipe, snatch, skid, slap, whizzing arms
and volleys, flying sweat, muttered curses.
The cops were as captivated as I was,
the first day any of us had seen
the game played without a ball.
No-ball Handball: and yet not one point,
not one out of bounds call was disputed.

And when Fortin finally put the game away,
punched in a shot that left what's-his-name
looking dumb and deflated, he walked over
dripping, breathless, gave the invisible ball
one more sharp bounce off the floor, and
to welcome any post-game commentary
greeted the cops with a triumphant,
awshucks-sportsmanship smile.
But the cops were already backing out
into the hallway, the last one
with his hands held chest high, a careful
pushing-off motion, a way of saying
Let's just... Just... Let's just... Let's
just... Just... Just let's...

Paul Violi

BLONDE ON BLONDE

It happens at a party, this way, past frat boys
perched in branches like idiot hoot owls,
past a painted girl with a plastic
beer cup and bangs like a dark waterfall
who promises you a new way to whisper.

Outside, on the porch, the neighbor,
or perhaps some strange antiquated refugee.
Grizzled, goat-faced, hippie guru in flannel,
he sits cross-legged near a turntable,
drops the needle just as you pass,
and you stop, startled by a noise like a man
stretching after so many years in a crouch.

The words, you think, could be stolen
verbatim from your deadbeat old man
as he sleeptalks the afternoon away,
one foot dangling off of the couch,
while the world of the gainfully employed
rotates in necessary cycles around
the tin box house the two of you live in.

Together, noise and words are like
doing a crossword puzzle while
standing in a joyous metallic rainshower,
like having a conversation with some
grander version of the sun.

Dylan, says the hippie, and suddenly you are
unafraid of difficult ideas or the dark.
You have been shaving your pink face
for, what, all of about three weeks now,
and yet, you find yourself suddenly mourning
the end of the long, bloody Trojan War,
the decimation of the age of Enlightenment.

From this point forward it will be difficult
to smell certain flowers or women
without wanting to become an outlaw.
You press your hand to your sunken chest
and curse the cruel passage of time
for stranding you in the one period
in all of this long lie called history
without room for heroism or holiness.

You bow your head and duck inside –
like, but never again exactly like, all
the vanished souls who went before.

Justin Hamm

LEAVING IT ALL BEHIND

A spotted leaf tags the window,
a snick of leopard skin. Someone across
the way draws an orange curtain
to keep their concentration in, maintain
the light that feeds their creativity,

the little red fish that swims round the head
all day before vision goes dead.
This someone designs hats,
a milliner's felt, surrealist games.
She lives with 13 cats.

There are so many bizarre impulses,
nerve messages transmitted everywhere
at every moment. And my food is blue
if eaten imaginatively,
marine colours, a turquoise artichoke,

a slice of dark blue bread.
Ideas are buzzing in the air,
and when the lightning crackles energy
translates the concept. It's a man-sized bee

I pass on the street into town,
the first, or are there others? A friend's poetry
evoked that image yesterday,
others may be sitting on park benches
the way French lovers do. A new species.

The orange curtain won't be drawn all day,
although I'll invent what happens behind
that screening. A woman and 13 cats.
The biggest one has one good eye, one eye blind.

Jeremy Reed

SAD EYED LADY

It inaugurates each empty room, each night
illuminated by 60 watts and candle flame,
this ritual: something old for something new.

Dylan's quaver, a minor key, a descent
down the scale. We sing together, not quite
in tune, one note held for years. I carry him

on worn-out cassettes, shiny discs; he resists
every advance, the stubborn scratch of his voice,
jangly tambourine, *oh sad eyed lady*

should I wait? He navigates me through
births and deaths, endless days of rain,
all the same to him, his song pressed

into vinyl long ago, a woman he loved,
an age; what has passed he has passed
to me, as I strike out beyond the parapet

of my teenage room, only to find the room
will never change; I am the same, just older,
my face transforming in the mirror.

Tamar Yoseloff

LOW LANDS

I often think of her, and him,
of course, without his drum
year after year. It's always late afternoon
in a landscape so flat that the eyes give up
trying to see as far as the horizon.
It is a place, perhaps below sea level.

Her home, though not by choice
and his accidental stopping place.
Packing and travelling and leaving
so many things behind.
He has small slips of paper
stuffed in pockets to remind him.

The storage tag says simply
'Arabian drum'. There is no mention
of whose hands are accustomed to its skin
or how he longs for the feel of it,
and the sound of its hollow tones.
Whose eyes are craving a glimpse
of this well decorated instrument?
It is just something left behind.

I think more about the drum than about them,
and more about the eyes than about the drum
and more about the sadness in the eyes
than about anything.
I see the black lines drawn all
around his eyes and I imagine
how long she must have looked at him.

Pencilled boldly like an Indian Prince,
a noble chief in war-paint, perhaps
a drag queen from Chicago,
the highlights of sadness, showing.
She has become like him,
quiet, not carrying much,
although she is at home.

Linda Chase

THE NIGHTINGALE'S CODE

She attempts a smile; the current tears at the stones
That strew its course, while overhead odd, waxy
Foliage glints in the sun. Beyond the grove voices
Are calling, calling the strayed members of numberless flocks;
They arrived, pock-marked and sleepless, muttering about
Ruin, and the tricks played by morning, and long
Forgotten routines. Our maps disagreed, until now
Only the awful and vacant remain yet
To be prised apart. I'd turned for home, hardly
Daring to breathe, as the highlighted zones declared war
On their meddlesome neighbours. I'd learned that silence
Lies in wait, then leaps to shroud the furniture. Grimacing,
The vowels retire, mass gloomily on the far
Horizons, where chalk and sand prepare to unfold
Their stiffened arms, to offer up their restive secrets.

Mark Ford

NIGHTWATCHMAN

For Bob Dylan

It was not you
followed me home whispering,
left a noose tidy on my doormat –

for you I lit a red light
lit the flame lit the gas
sat on the winter sill

looked out at the night
city of smoking tips, flicker
of insomniacs

and drinking was one option
for rubbing out my face
but you were the other –

you growled from the heat
calling in the pipes, ghost
of electricity and angers,

my grief in your throat
horse-rhythm I could feel where bone
meets soul: I was where,

in lone dark, through opposite lights
so bald and hot, your face flared
to transparency across their distance,

I could almost see you, and see you now,
looking back, still watching over me.

Pippa Little

A WURLITZER IN ANNAGARY

A bar that used to be a laundromat
that used to be a chipper with a Wurlitzer
in the times when – imagine that.
Or a Wurlitzer in Lucy's Tiger Den,
the last of the Nam bars holding out
in the City of Angels, can you hear
that lit-up Wurlitzer playing tonight?
Or remember Cindy's diner in Duluth
that overlooked the Iron Range,
where you turned up in dungarees
and donkey jacket, tucked a Lucky
behind an ear with ink-stained fingers
bitten to the quick, and mimed a Little Richard
hip-gyration that didn't quite come off?
Imagine that winter of fifty-six
lost among the mining towns where
a sinkhole Wurlitzer is holding down
a vinyl payload sunk beyond repair,
or better still a Wurlitzer that spins
and lifts and drops and plays that thing
like copters in the jungle, like whirligigs
letting go their load for Charlie.
I offer you tonight a Wurlitzer of air
where once the Border Ballads were,
where vinyl spins and plays that thing,
a Wurlitzer of song and times gone wrong,
of times long gone on the Iron Range,
of Vietnam jungle and Annagary chipper,
a Wurlitzer in 1967 when I was eleven.

Padraig Rooney

TWO POEMS FOR BOB DYLAN'S SEVENTIETH BIRTHDAY

1

Cordelia

Asked by the King my Father to praise Bob Dylan
I found no words   nothing to say to praise him
whose fame is vast   who is honoured in every country
whose songs are like Constellations
in the night of Egypt or the Randan Woods

2

The Old Woodland Yew

> *strap yourself*
> *to the tree with roots*
> *   you ain't goin' nowhere*

I come to the old woodland yew
when the frost is sprinkled like powder on the leaves
and the sun is a bright fiery seed.

He is in a quiet corner by the second pool
and I greet him with caution, respectfully,
by walking nine times around him.

He allows me to enter and rest in his fork.
His branches are extremely flexible.
His strength is pre-industrial.

His roots are anchored deep
in leaf mould and the sandy soil
where foxes and young badgers in the spring

are watched by curious naturalists
who've rigged up lights among the trees.
I listened for a message:

The Yew asked me to come more often
and if I remembered the story of the fox
whose tail dangled in the well and froze.

I asked him his age:
He said four hundred years.
I left the yew walking in the direction of the sun
stumbling over foxholes.

Christopher Twigg

CLOTHES LINE

I called, you didn't answer your phone.
At first I didn't mind very much.
I went outside to take in the clothes,
your socks were sopping wet to the touch.
Wendy came over, she wanted some eggs.
She asked what the music was.
I said 'Clothes Line Saga', it's brilliant, it's Bob.
Then I rang you again just because
the signal was good. You didn't reply.
I put out three shirts on the line.
It was December the thirteenth,
Monday. Everything seemed fine.

I rang you again, you didn't answer,
so I rang the office number at school.
The secretary said she'd pass the message on,
she sounded stressed, but not exactly rude.
The dogs were barking at my neighbour outside
'Is that the radio?' she said, 'Heard the news?
The main road's closed, the traffic's gone mad.'
The dogs played around by the hose.
I said, 'Oh well, I don't have to go out.
It's something I can forget.'
I went round the back with a basket of pegs
to see if your shirts were still wet.

I turned off the music, I folded the shirts.
I thought I'd take the dogs for a walk.
I thought I'd send you a text
but didn't, I only really wanted to talk.
I was still half asleep, full of the week-end,
I didn't really have a lot to say.
A police car pulled up and a policeman
got out. He said, 'Are you Ann Gray?'
He said, 'Could I come in?'
I said, 'Yes, of course.'
I went into the house, and Wendy met me.
And then I shut all the doors.

Ann Gray

LET ME FOLLOW YOU DOWN

you   casting shadows the size of an ocean with your pet stiletto
crooked pin smile skulker in the reeds minus oxygen blackcurrant
vodka drainpipes cadging a snifter from the scally in the stars
above cupping truth against the breeze from the emperor's tent

you   won't give yourself away Mister Bitter Mystery not to Mona
Prince Skin 'n' Bones not to old Professor Trix plying you with
neat Tennyson & Keats not to Miss Priss Honeypie Singalong not
to the King of America not to Achilles on the run on the lookout
for hard cash a new deal an exchange of goodwill out walking the
dog

you   have you heard the one about the last man standing about a
shadow fingering your collar about the shape of a flint-tip spear
about the size of an ocean it will follow you the rest of your life

Peter Carpenter

BLUE GOSSIP

I guess he got sick of having to get up and get
          scared of being shot down
Also probably he got sick of
          being a methedrine clown;
Also he wanted to go back explore
          Macdougal Street New York town

I guess he got sick of a Cosmic
          consciousness too abstract
I guess he wanted to go back
          t'his own babies' baby shit fact
Change his own children's diapers not get lost
          in a transcendental Rock & Roll act.

I guess he thought maybe he had
          enough gold for the world
Saw red white & blue big enough now
          needn't be further unfurled
I guess he felt prophet show good example,
          bring himself down in the world.

I guess he took Zen Chinese vows
          and became an anonymous lout
I guess he figured he better step down off stage
          before he got kicked out
I guess he felt lonesome and blue
          and he wanted out.

I guess he did what anyone
          sens'ble would do
Otherwise like Mick Jagger go out on stage
          wearing curtains of blue
And fly around the world with great big
          diamonds and pearls made of glue.

I guess he felt he'd used up
            'nuff of the 'lectric supply
I guess he know that the Angel
            of Death was nigh –
I guess he sighed his
            next mortal sigh.

I guess he guessed he could
            find out his own mortal face
I guess he desired to examine
            his own family place
I guess he decided to act with
            more modest silent grace

I guess he decided to learn
            from ancient tongue
So he studied Hebrew
            as before he babbled from his lung
I guess he required to learn new
            tender kind songs to be sung.

I guess he thought he was not guru
            for Everyone's eyes
He must have seen Vajra Hells
            in old visions he'd divined
He must've seen infernal assassins
            stealing his garbage supplies.

I guess he decided to die
            while still alive
In that way, ancient death-in-life,
            saint always thrive
Above all remember his children
            he already picked a good wife.

I guess he decided to Be
          as well as sing the blues
I guess he decided like Prospero
          to throw his white magic wand into the
               Ocean blue –
Burn up all is magic books,
          go back to Manhattan, think something new.

I guess he decided like Prospero
          World was a dream
Every third thought is grave
          or so Samsara would seem –
Took Hebrew Bodhisattva's vow
          and saw golden light death agleam.

I guess he decided he
          did not need to be More Big
I guess he decided he was not the
          Great Cosmic Thingamajig
I guess he decided to end that sweet song
          and such is his Suchness I dig.

Allen Ginsberg
23 October 1972, Davidson College

ODE

for Bob Dylan

MY EYES ARE WIDE EXPLOSIONS
in the field of nowhere.
My pocketwatch burns air
and sprouts golden antlers.
I'm
the stand-in
for flaming stars;
my heart murmurs
are electric guitars
and
my hair
reflects in rainbows
and in aura glows
that radiate my brow.
The tinsel ice
does melt
beneath my feet –
my words are fleet –
and my songs
are an armada.
I see
the smiles of cherubs float
from the barranca.
The world with all its facets
is a whirling boat
of leopards and of mice
from which I hurl
the radiant dice
of my perceptions.
All conceptions
of boundaries
are lies!

Michael McClure

THE JACK OF HEARTS

for Dylan

Who are we now, who are we ever,
Skin books parchment bodies libraries of the living
gilt almanachs of the very rich
encyclopedias of little people
packs of player face down
on faded maps of America
with no Jack of Hearts
in the time of the ostrich
Fields full of rooks
dumb pawns in black and white kingdoms
And revolutions the festivals of the oppressed
and festivals the little revolutions
of the bourgeoisie
where gypsy fortune tellers deal
without the Jack of Hearts
the black-eyed one who sees all ways
the one with the eye of a horse
the one with the light in his eye
the one with his eye on the star named Nova
the one for the ones with no one to lead them
the one whose day has just begun
the one with the star in his cap
the cat with future feet
looking like a Jack of Hearts
mystic Jack Zen Jack with crazy koans
Vegas Jack who rolls the bones
the high roller behind the dealer
the one who'll shake them
the one who'll shake the ones unshaken
the fearless one
the one without bullshit
the stud with the straightest answer
the one with blazing words for guns
the distance runner with the word to pass

the night rider with the urgent message
The man from La Mancha riding bareback
The one who bears the great tradition
and breaks it
The Mysterious Stranger who comes & goes
The Jack of Hearts who speaks out
in the time of the ostrich
the one who sees the ostrich
the one who sees what the ostrich sees in the sand
the one who digs the mystery
and stands in the corner smiling
like a Jack of Hearts
at the ones with no one to lead them
the ones with their eyes in the sands
the sand that runs through the glass
the ones who don't want to look
at what's going down around them
the shut-eye ones who wish
that someone else would seize the day
that someone else would tell them
which way up and which way out
and whom to hate and whom to love
like Big Jack groovy Jack the Jack of light
Sainted Jack who had the Revelations
and spoke the poem of apocalypse
Poet Jack with the light pack
who travels by himself
and leaves the ladies smiling
Dharma Jack with the beatitudes
drunk on a bus addressing everyone
the silent ones with the frozen faces
the ones with The Wall Street Journal
who never speak to strangers
the ones that got lost in the shuffle
and never drew the Jack of Hearts
the one who'd turn them on
who'd save them from themselves
the one who heals the Hamlet in them

the silent Ham who never acts
the dude on the corner in two-tone shoes
who knows the name of the game
and names his game
the kid who paints the fence
the boy who digs the treasure up
the boy with the beans on the beanstalk
the dandy man the candy man
the one with the lollipops
the harlequin man
who tells the tic-toc man to stuff it
in front of the house that Jack built
where sleeps the Cock that crowed in the morn
where sleeps the Cow with the crumpled horn
where sleeps the dude who kept the horse
with the beautiful form
and kissed the Maiden all forlorn
the Jack of the pack all tattered and torn
the one the queen keeps her eye on
Dark Rider on a white horse
after the Apocalypse
Prophet stoned on the wheel of fortune
Sweet singer with harp half-hid
who speaks with the cry of cicadas
who tells the tale too truly
for the ones with no one to tell them
the true tale of sound and fury
the Jack of Hearts who lays it out
who tells it as it is
the one who wears no watch
yet tells the time too truly
and reads the Knight of Cups
and knows himself
the Knave of Hearts the Jack of Hearts
who stole the tarts
of love & laughter
the Jack who tells his dream
to those with no one to dream it

the one who tells his dream
to the hard-eyed innocents
and lays it out for the blind hippie
the black dream the white dream
of the Jack of Hearts
whose skeleton is neither black nor white
the long dream the dream of heads & hearts
the trip of hearts the flip of hearts
that turns the Hanged Man right side up
and saves the Drowned Sailor
with the breath of love
the wet dream the hard dream the sweet dream
of the Deck Hand on the tall ship sailing softly
Blackjack yellowjack the steeplejack
who sets the clock in the tower
and sees the chimes of freedom flashing
his only watch within him
the high one the turned-on one the tuned-in one
the one who digs
in the time of the ostrich
and finds the sun-stone
of himself
the woman-man
the whole man
who holds all worlds together
when all is said and all is done
in the wild eye the wide eye
of the Jack of Hearts
who stands in a doorway
clothed in sun

Lawrence Ferlinghetti

LEGACY

I leave you the green silk dress that wasn't silk
but shivered like it was, slipped easy as an arm
around a neck for the last slow dance at a go-down
jazz club night; I leave you a chiffon scarf

and Chemistry, the chill of the attic room we chafed in,
the basements full of strangers-into-friends
and the fire that blazed in the last one, one September
to come home to, weary, punch-drunk, bundle-laden.

I leave you the strange enthusiastic neighbour,
expert in the ways of trains and traffic lights,
and the jazz man with no sense of rhythm, the lie
of perfect pitch, our syncopating spoons and bones.

I leave you a singer with too many words to the line,
who made them fit and mean between the wheeze of
chords,
the thrill of sitting there not shouting *Judas* while
the others upped and left. I leave you poetry & jazz,

the angst of anger, bears & squirrels, the kitchen sink
of cinema, the grainy grey of subtitles, the books
we'd *really read* piled round the edge of the room,
that rug, those ankle-bruising chairs, the suck of wind

that slammed the door, that smashed the glass, the sound
as it shattered, fell, the pick of our bare feet through it.

Susan Utting

TANGLED UP IN BLUE

He said he wanted us to see
all of Tangled Up In Blue
at the same time –
past, present, future
entwined as though
it's all happening
simultaneously, her
with the red hair
and he with his itinerant job
in Delacroix.

And now this from last
month's New Scientist:

*"The apparent boundaries between past, present and future are only
illusions caused by the amount of action you can physically per-
ceive, and so it seems to you that one moment exists and is gone
forever, and the next moment comes and like the one before also dis-
appears."*

She is reading from a book
by a thirteenth-century Italian
poet, yet she is also
present at the moment
of that book's
conception.

The shoe-laces she ties
form an infinity symbol,
from me to you.

The burner she lights
on the stove
is the sun as it expands and
goes slowly
supernova.

Glenn Cooper

PLUTARCH

So that poet from the 13th century
was Plutarch?
A full verse was axed.
When she bent
to tie your shoelace,
her breasts showed, briefly.
Then you took a freight train
out of context.

Two bars on harmonica,
then fade.
Her folks disapproved
of your mother's hemlines
and the decree nisi was late.
That car was left *out west*.
Your affair had no
middle 8.

Now all your relationships
worsen.
You were sea-sick
on that boat to Delacroix.
In his basement flat
you swapped cigarettes with his slaves,
then left
in the third person.

Matthew Caley

IF YOU SEE HER

Those familiar minor sixths unspool
from the wheels of the cracked tape
that motors this small car, wrapping
round the cogs of this long year.

Your voice breaks over this crease of hill
and in this evening a rusted cut throat
pares a slice of improbable sky.
She is not in Tangiers and I've no rhyme

to match up like washed socks. So I nod
hello, to the scatter of birds, like black
crayon kisses blown across a scrawl of sky.
And here, with Ribblesdale spread

below me like the footprint of Minnesota,
you offer me the kingdoms of the world.

Edward Mackay

MIDWINTER ARMISTICE

The radio says *Thaw* –
water drips from eaves
and broken gutters.
Some time past midnight,
snow's duvet shrugs itself
from the roof, slips past
our window and now
lies below us, slumped
over the clipped yews.

Blood on the Tracks,
stuck on repeat, backs
the intermittent crashing
of icicles and falling coals,
rain's neat fingering
on upturned milk-pails
and our two pulses
beating together
just out of sync.

Staying up late again
in a brief heady truce
stoked by shared joints,
we lie back by the fire,
tangled up and too spaced
out to see we always did
feel the same – but hey,
now it's from a
different point of view

Angela Kirby

ACQUIESCENCE

Apparently, we crossed that tawdry snowline
to come upon a lynx in an ice-hung hawthorn, then another,
                                        or the same one again
by a lightning-struck pine.
The cold was a presence.
When the dog squatted to pee
its pee became a little sheeted lake. By an icicle-fringed gulley
Fontainbleau let slip about the bodies,
and a little further up we found a cairn, then an improvised
                                        sepulchre.
We prised the biggest slab but nothing grinned back at us –
                                        just foetid air.

Without jewellery, descending through dank copses I thought of
                                        Clytemnestra,
the pearl-string glimmering on her chest,
how amongst the All-Nite girls from the Mobil garage, none
                                        could best her

for heft or malevolence. Our furs became coral. The cold grew
                                        inside us like a worm.
The dog died trying to shit a snowball. The gulley took its whine.
A warm voice called out to us. It felt like acquiescence.

                                        Matthew Caley

63

AMERICAN CLIP

FREEWHEELIN' BOB DYLAN
       TURANDOT AND OTHER POEMS
THE TIMES THEY ARE A-CHANGIN'
       SOME TREES
BRINGING IT ALL BACK HOME
       THE TENNIS COURT OATH
HIGHWAY 61 REVISITED
       RIVERS AND MOUNTAINS
BLONDE ON BLONDE
       THE DOUBLE DREAM OF SPRING
NASHVILLE SKYLINE
       A NEST OF NINNIES
NEW MORNING
       THREE POEMS
PLANET WAVES
       THE VERMONT NOTEBOOK
BLOOD ON THE TRACKS
       SELF-PORTRAIT IN A CONVEX MIRROR
STREET LEGAL
       HOUSEBOAT DAYS

Rachelle Bijou

FROM THE BOOK OF PRAISES

(of Bob Dylan)

Moon blowing away like a dandelion;
Radio wavers, bounced off Orion with codes
Of its own. The song says there's roads
In this hole, where a hound sounds like iron.

Bowlegged old men carry in the bone
The suffering children from Chi-town to Rome
To Biloxi, pellagra and rickets and lice.
The toll of their hardships got caught in your backwoods
voice.

Across the fields you point out
The burnt shell of your father's house.

Silence, rain, the road not going nowhere, going away…
Blackbird singing on the Red Wing wall…
Two lanes of 61, St Paul to Thunder Bay…
Mercury glints on grass. Lightning's eastbound scrawl.

John Gibbens

BEFORE THE ROAD SHOW

huge pine coffins
slide across the boards
disgorge equipment

cables writhe
two men kick
a roll of carpet
into flat submission

a technician
unpacks a piano
floods the stage
with Scarlatti
no one turns around

three mouths mate
one microphone

phrases float parallel
a shout dissects
'how many hats d'you need?'

a groupie
purple tyres
under her eyes
picks up a truck driver
leaves her friend behind

swathed in a red kimono
one foot curling a thigh
she chips scarlet lacquer
from her big toe
says being in love
beats loneliness

Ginsberg and Dylan
stroll the local bone orchard
quoting Apollinaire

a Mexican girl
in a wedding dress
hums an Indian song

tongues beckon
caress like leopard slugs

a pregnant dancer
silhouettes in the mirror
calls for a second opinion

fingers indulge surfaces
sing round wine glasses

a dark woman stacks fortunes
explores the tracery of palms
turns up the eight of spades
reshuffles the pack
deals a fair boy
in the queen of clubs   and winks
runs a long finger
slowly under his lips

in a corner
girls with kohl-rimmed eyes
define each other's faces

a boy naked but for a halo
and skeletal wings
inclines leonine curls
to his violin
three singers link hands
perform a mock pavane

the girl who never speaks
laces her white chemise
balances a tiny bottle
between her knees
paints her fingernails blue

nobody knows how long
this train's been travelling

Patricia Pogson

THE LAST WALTZ

Death underwrites their music's dignity,
The bogey-man of living on the road,
That lends their rock its dark alacrity,
A music turned by men who know what's owed.
Their genial modesty does not preclude
The litany of Janis, Jimi, Brian;
The doped eyes' morbid twinkle only proves
If they're not dead, it's not for want of trying.

When Dylan comes on ripping songs to bits,
The cognoscenti aren't in any doubt
He's doing it because they once were hits,
Which justifies his nasal torture-bouts.
This is the way the Abendland goes down,
The lamp's flame spitting in the mirror's eye;
There's no-one worth a flattering glance in town,
Though somehow hirsute millionaires get by.

Then just to prove it's all about salvation,
He tunes his voice for 'I Shall Be Released',
The universal prisoner's declaration
That lends this evening's sense of ending peace.
The slow refrain is raised by rock musicians,
Steel-driving rhythms eased to navigate
The waters of prospective manumission
Where history and hard travelling terminate.

Douglas Houston

AT EARLS COURT AND ELSEWHERE

An etiolated pale figure too surrounded
By darkness, distant: to leave the cheap seats early
In search of the bar, it seemed more in the spirit
Of his thing.
            Sang instead his songs on the Tube
Almost back to Bob the Wop's in Limehouse,
Until a grinning stranger invited me to his party
The next week: to shut me up, perhaps; or the quark
And charm that alone make life. I never went.
Never heard him in concert again either. As, once,
My mind sparking still with acid from the night
Before, I set forth that Christmas Day morning
Down snowy Winterton Road, Kingstanding, *Bringing
It All Back Home* under my arm, and went
Searching for some radiant guardian friend (it
Was my radiant guardian friend).
                      She,
You might add, was a girl from the North Country, he
Came in out of some storm. They shared the road
A space until the goads that sent them there
Drove them apart. For that time, though, more
Than human, less than beasts, and yet
You could not call it love. What more is there
Anyone can ever say? You may call
The howling moon as witness, take a last
Cup of coffee, listen to the linnet singing sweet
In its high registers, yet not deny it. Righteous
To avoid righteousness at the last,
As the cold around the distinct heat draws in.

John Goodby

AERODROME

Don't talk of the words that were lost on the wind,
the multitude prone on the tarmac, his voice
like the voice from a distant echoing cave,
our one hundred thousand cheap lighters raised
like an answering beacon, the uncanny shimmer
surrounding his head, the death of the moon.

Remind me instead of the tongues of fire
we saw by the roadside that night, the visions
that curled like snakes from our tangled hair,
the veteran flight-sergeant, burning coals
in his eyes, who stopping to give us a ride
told us *Write of the things thou hast seen*

and drove down the A31 on the flaming wings
of an eagle, our low hills and dark world revealed.

Jane Draycott

THE SAN DIEGO CROSS

When he gave protest the finger
I gave protest the finger
Pointed my finger
At those finger pointers
Mailed dead men's fingers
To *Sing Out!* magazine
Ate Tom Paxton's hat

When he discovered electricity
I discovered electricity
Burned my zither collection
Took a sharp axe
To Pete Seeger's banjo
Plugged myself in
Til my ears smoked blue

And when he got God good
I got God bad
Drank the juice of the Vineyard
Played the Signs and Wonders
In Chuck and Larry's band
Filched that silver cross
From the preacher man's pants...

Up here on Thunder Mountain
In my missionary hut
Reading *Missionary Times*
I'm playing *Saved* on my 8-track
I've got an eight track mind
And three of them are Dylan's
And five of them are mine

Nathaniel Blue

DIGESTING CRAB CLAWS

'Don't fall apart on me tonight...'
The tape's up loud, and Dylan's back
from the Crusades, and we sit
half a mile from the frothed Atlantic,
digesting a bucket of crab claws
as the sea wind tests the putty.
An hour now and we haven't stirred
from this table, except to change
the tape, and feed the range
that eats turf like a generator
though its back boiler is holed.
And I pulled on the anorak
to go for turf, past the line
where a blue flag of jeans
makes the pegs earn their keep,
and back inside, I spoke
of slates that scythed down,
and of snapped-off branches.
No-one listened. They stared out
at the would-be mountain opposite,
as if someone scuttled there
wearing red, past the houses,
then their upwardly errant sheep,
to stand, hunched, on the ridge
with the cairn and the tv booster
barely visible to us below.

Matthew Sweeney

YOUNGER THAN THAT NOW

Open the door one crack and you are backstage.
The closest of the urgently silent faces
Is amber-dark, but away down the crowded passage
They get much gloomier, longer to recognise
      Your shyly whispered guesses.

Widen and die like cigarette fumes in a hall
Of cleanly livers. You did not know you were holding
Your breath till it broke clear and there is no wall
To touch, there are only inhabited crackling clothes
      And soon the dizzying feeling

That you must walk through here through the way of them all,
The girls of the frozen chorus, the mouthing page,
The hero blank, the jacketed devil, the cool
Chanel of the goddess, the flirt o'the woods; pass on
      Away from the terrible stage

That grinds its young in the light or blows them dark
Like birthday candles, moves down corridors
Where the murdered glance from a brilliant mirror and back,
By vast and icy rooms with bills of plays
      That call you to old wars,

Past centuries of dresses coldly hung
In line, rich girls speechless at the affront,
And cards of luck and photographs of song
Pinned to a blistered board, pass by the wires
      That lead from what you want

Away to the grids and terminals of power,
Pass by yourself in brown and broken glass,
By planks and crates at the foot of a storage tower,
By what seems rubbish to you but will be of use,
      And then the rubbish. Pass

Right to the end of the theatre, some last
Green paint-spattered chair by a bolted door.
Far from the lives of the sad, superior cast,
Or earshot of their over-expressing lines,
        Sit yourself down there.

Feel like a boy the burden tremble and slip.
Empty your pockets of work and empty your ears
And nose and eyes of fashion. Summon up
Whatever remains. If nothing remains amen.
        But blink no appealing tears,

For here you sit in the foreground of the world.
And what you play in the dark is the plain song
Of men alone: unobservant, innocent, old
And blue with wonder, and beating a way back home
        And over before long.

                        Glyn Maxwell

FROM THE HILL OF MUSES

Philopappos – Athens – June 1989

Where scorched earth traps the divine,
Dylan and Van, busking in time
above drained beds of river soils
and dried up swamps,
joined in songs whose strings hold on
to pain and whatever passes
down lanes to where the past ever was,
Bob's left-handed harp blowing choruses
through a foreign window
Byron opened one scented night ago –
where worn trails of travellers, either still
in sight or a long way gone,
can take what shelter in the air
remains in The Parthenon –
both deemed wiser now – as the light of day
puts the burden in their eyes a mere heart beat away –
from an age below whose columns above
were weighed down and stoned by crazy love
from the front of the stage to the back of the throat:
     a singer delivers this single note
     that still isn't over
     and wraps you in glory –
     Tell me your story?

Phil Bowen

ELOQUENCE

after 'Dignity' – Bob Dylan

Nowhere man sitting in a silent room
History man thinking of Pharaoh's tomb
Clergyman talking to the bride and groom
With eloquence

Worried man looking for a wounded saint
Handyman opening a can of paint
Hipster man digging what certainly ain't
Like eloquence

Someone got married on Christmas Day
Someone said eloquence gave them away
I went into the village – sat in the inn –
Saw the land of the harvest moon

Seeking here – seeking there
Seeking almost everywhere
Asking the teachers who once used to care
About eloquence

Wanted man wandering right from the start
Puts all his desires inside his heart
Wonders if there's any kind of counterpart
For eloquence

I went to the funeral of Jukebox Jones
They said: 'we don't like your sticks and stones'
Had heard too much on their telephones
About eloquence

I headed down to where the wild dogs roam
Would have turned round quicker if I thought it meant home
Saw the eyes of sorrow in a bridal gown
Seemed like the same old single road

Chilli hot sun as a mouth on fire
Land all flooded – rent got higher
Going to walk to the front ask the head of the choir
Has he heard eloquence?

Winning man looking at his crowning years
In a stadium of light full of drowning cheers
Hearing all those half-remembered fears
About eloquence

Said goodbye to Queen Maggie in The Twisted Wheel
She placed coins on the counter for the price of the meal
Put her hands in her pockets – said she wasn't going to kneel
To eloquence

White gloves wiping the window pane
Trees all bent – slow mud on the lane
I met the daughters of night and the daughters of day
In the highway cities of gloom

Got no room to hide – got no walking shoes
Miss Lonely cried when she heard the news
Reading between the lines and the Ps and Qs
Of eloquence

Strong man staring in his trainer's eyes
Looking at the weight – the shape and the size
And any conceivable kind of compromise
For eloquence

Frenchman writing on a long slow boat
Plucks his guitar – hums this single note
Looks at the words he still hasn't wrote
On eloquence

Someone took me to the home of Barnaby Brown
He said eloquence has never been written down
I read into the green – sped right through the red
Into headlamps of dead-end pain

So there's one last no and one last yes
One last man standing, more or less
Sometimes I wonder will anyone confess
To eloquence

Miles Wilder

THE BOOTLEG SERIES

He was still raving about Dylan's
The Bootleg Series months later.
He'd had his season in hell
though the Devil still visited
from time to time in the form
of sounds from the street.

His ex would call on Saturdays,
drop off their daughter. He'd play
The Bootleg Series and try
to get Christine to eat something.
She was between one and a half and two.
It's a funny age to be,

a funny one to watch.
She cheered him up when the grilling
he'd had from the detectives
started to get him down,
remembering the ice bath.
The Bootleg Series cheered him up too.

The Bootleg Series was playing
the day the lawyers' letter came
telling him to forget it,
he was in poverty and would be
as long as his name wasn't
formerly Robert Allen Zimmerman,

The Bootleg Series his latest release,
bringing together strands
from a brilliant thirty-year career
– Christine could even dance
to parts of it, danced her dolls too
and joined in here and there.

So he traded in his mouth organ
for a fountain pen and got a job
writing job applications for people
who couldn't write their own
for some reason. He'd have gone nuts
if it wasn't for *The Bootleg Series*.

The year went past uneventfully.
His nails grew again,
his only pleasures in life
were *The Bootleg Series* and beer.
He put a little weight on,
took lessons in opening his mouth

without offending someone.
Christmas was a bastard of course,
but by the new year he was
fully re-charged, ready to move.
He packed *The Bootleg Series*,
took a boat and finished up

eating pizza at a table
by the Med. *The Bootleg Series*
found new fans in the soldiers
who visited him in the room
where he cut the deals. He made
a killing and got out quick,

bought a house with the profits
in the remotest place he could think of.
Things drifted in and out of favour,
he found God, then lost Him,
but never at any point stopped
listening to *The Bootleg Series*.

Geoff Hattersley

40TH BIRTHDAY WITH CASSETTE
DECK AND QUESTIONS

In the next room children come and go,
talking of Michelangelo
and other awesome dudes.
O'Driscoll is on his knees again,
deciding which cut of *One Too Many Mornings*
to dub for the party tapes.

Is that a smell of burning?

He settles for an upbeat country treatment
from the Isle of Wight bootleg.
The blue-jeaned tolerant original
they'd be embarrassed by. And he's not ready yet
for the leather-coated stand-off of *Hard Rain*.

Should he risk a white suit?

Beginning a slow bowler's windmill
to ease his stiff shoulder,
he remembers a song of Pete Townshend's.
The line *I was just 34 years old*.

Will anybody come?

Tim Dooley

FANCY MAN

Get to him late through another man's
            tapes.

Fancy him there
            thumbing gut.
Side of the road.

Want some gum?

Guardians left
            chasing up wires.

Foot down. Climb high.
Go.

Jowls of words
            in the rearview mirror
                    could cradle
but catch fire
            in sad-eyed woods.

A phrase is given a bit of length and flicked
                all the way to the mic.

            and on.
Coming back down
            flat
                as old moonlight.
Jack up the car.
Change the wheel.

            Spacey in the wind.

        No hurry

           getting anywhere

        I want.

Mary Maher

DYLANNELLE

Mr tambourine man, if not for you
blowin' in the wind, you could still be mine.
Looks like it's all over now, baby blue.

You made me feel just like a woman, you
angel you, a hurricane down my spine,
Mr tambourine man. If not for you

and your subterranean homesick blues,
knocking on heaven's door, wanting a sign...
Looks like it's all over now, baby blue.

Blonde on blonde, under a red sky, we flew.
My desire, my gates of Eden would shine,
My tambourine man, if not for you.

But you got yourself tangled up in blue
and love minus zero was your cool line.
Looks like it's all over now, baby blue.

Blood on the tracks, good as I been to you,
Most likely you'll go your way, I'll go mine,
Mr tambourine man, if not for you.
Looks like it's all over now, baby blue.

Linda France

FINE BY ME

Dylan Ghazal for Mimi Khalvati

Bob, if you want to talk that's fine by me.
What I've just thought of is a line by me.

If Klute's Cradle was still here in Camden,
In a corner light you could dine by me

And Mimi. And we could gaze at dark skies,
Whose angel eyes are all divine by me.

This crazy high street is crowded outside.
But here is a space for you to sign by me.

And no, not discuss any cures for love
Or pain – just to sit and drink wine by me

And Mimi – don't worry about what's left
On the train – I'll keep it with mine by me.

And if Mimi says: 'if you want to write
Me a song,' then write eight or nine by me.

I've no grounds for complaint, as Hafez says,
'Isn't any song Bob writes fine by me.'

Anon after Hafez

SHOOTING STAR

'I seen a shooting star tonight, and I thought of you...'

In a San Francisco basement apartment
There's a woman I keep hearing about, who
Claims for the last twenty years she's lived
With Bob Dylan, and wishes to write a book about it.
That might mostly be new to him – *hey man,*
You must be putting me on. But she sells scarves
From her own North Beach shop, and according
To this woman Dylan's changed – a lot –
Heavy now, yet kind, if also a little
Crazy, in and out of hospitals, he doesn't look
Like himself. Still, wherever he travels
He mails her love poems in his familiar
60s style, and she'd be honored to show them around.

A sleepy kitchen at dawn, the woman steps
Towards the kettle, pajamas open to her waist,
An owlish man, drunken, slothful, lags behind.
The glamour of the damaged, but how much
More gratifying for her not to have spun the whole
Hazy farrago out of loneliness, madness, or for money,
And this morning to wake beside someone
Who persuades you he recorded 'Shooting Star' just for
you.

Robert Polito

DON'T THINK TWICE

You didn't have the words
so used Bob's instead. *This
is how I feel*, you said.
I listened out for the lyric,
unsure if you meant all of it –
no use to sit and wonder why.

We were in the living room –
strange that – for months
I'd sat there in the dark,
prayed you might die, that
I could leave without telling you –
no use turning on the light.

That summer the grass dried up
on our lawn. Later, a New Year party,
the theme silver, I went 1920s style –
long gloves, cigarette holder,
opened my legs to a stranger
in a strange garden, where gravel

grated the skin on my shoulders
and somewhere there were whoops
and fireworks. My new millennium,
after two thirds of a bottle of whisky
I was too numb to care –
I'm not saying he treated me unkind.

Whereas, you knew
I was too young, that sixteen
and forty-five shouldn't add up.
You didn't love a woman, but a child.
This loveless shag, the only way
to make you leave me.

I was on the dark side, gave him
a necklace of blood bites, a gift
for his girlfriend, while the strings
of my heart-guitar hit E minor.
I told you when I was half sober,
naked from the shower,

and it was only half light outside.
You laid me on my back, hovered
over me, kissed the ridge
of bone, cupped my mound,
marked your territory. Stupidly,
I loved you more than ever

as you reclaimed and fucked me
from behind, not wanting to see
my face. I was sixteen, shamed,
while you, a married man, screwed
your daughter's friend –
goodbye's too good a word.

Suzanne Conway

BOB DYLAN AT PRINCETON, NOVEMBER 2000

We cluster at one end, one end of the Dillon Gym.
'You know what, honey? We call that a homonym.'

We cluster at one end, one end of the Dillon Gym.
'If it's fruit you're after, you go out on a limb.'

That last time in Princeton, that ornery degree,
those seventeen year locusts hanging off the trees.

That last time in Princeton, that ornery degree,
his absolute refusal to bend the knee.

His last time in Princeton, he wouldn't wear a hood.
Now he's dressed up as some sort of cowboy dude.

That last time in Princeton, he wouldn't wear a hood.
'You know what honey, we call that disquietude.

It's that selfsame impulse to rearrange
both "The Times They Are A-Changin" and "Things Have
Changed"

so that everything seems to fall within his range
as the locusts lock in on grain silo and grange.'

Paul Muldoon

THE VOICE

A voice, after closing-time,
is singing outside the prison wall,
within earshot of the cells,
a voice from another country,
singing without knowing,
a voice in the habit of crazy acts
and familiar with buckets of rain.

A voice that might have been a voice,
it sings across the brittle night,
after the inquests of dreams begin,
suddenly dropping, like glass onto stone,
from a high note to a low one.

Tears become luminous at its feet
before, protesting, it moves on.

Paul Henry

DYLAN, BOB AND ME

White Horse Tavern, New York. St David's Day 2002.

There's a white horse standing in a meadow
somewhere, and always three steps away
from everything else, and that's not far.
And no-one's asking 'Why the long face?'
Why should they when he's got
his own brand of whisky, got his own bar
where the poet looks down from his mural,
listens for scraps, today gets Clancey on how
Bobby took the village by storm. DT
wonders about a bourbon of his own:
'Could always call it *Eighteen Straight*...'

Half a century on, it's me, riding in
on the back of Dylan's fame, Bob's too.
The Welsh build him up to knock him down,
but tonight the boys are back in town, playing
up to the Rimbaud of Cwmdonkin,
as tales still flow tall in the Tavern,
and we're with Woody, Lomax, Leadbelly, Behan,
know the words to all the songs: 'These guys
are from Wales' and the free beers fly

past the actor playing Thomas who gets locked outside the bar,
but he'll go places – from The Gaslight to The Sidewalk,
then The Kettle, The Bitter End, all the way back
to Swansea's Old Guildhall – there's always somewhere
where it all just works, for a while. But sooner
or later it all falls out of style, comes a time
when it doesn't make much sense, when you have to start
moving back to your roots, relocate the point,
get on some other road, find yourself another joint....

David Woolley

SONG FOR BOB DYLAN

1971

The restless little
Midwestern creature
with reflecting eyes
tingling antennae
& scraping cry
secretes himself in
a new myth for each
winter & then drops
out & wings away
to another tree just
as his followers
begin to wriggle
in the cocoon
that's fallen behind

Norbert Krapf

FOUR VERSIONS OF A
RELATIONSHIP

Inspired by Todd Haynes' movie I'm Not There,
about the music, lives and times of Bob Dylan.

You are Charlotte Gainsbourg in a film.
I am two daughters with my brave faces.
You are Charlotte in her dressing gown

holding a cereal box. I'm an airport pilot.
We are not together when Vietnam ends.

Plan D

I am heavily eye-shadowed woman in
neck-brace. You're that 27 yr old boy
shoulder glued to book-shelf smoking

possessively in my direction. I'm café
booth look deepest, leave first. You lie
never with words. It starts to get iffy

about 3rd day, Cold-iron house with hot
exploding boiler, four eyes try hide it all,
I predict 'abounding' sensation. Lay on.

Plan C

Abstract toasts 'Here's to looking around more'
My puppet strings. Damn your suction boots
Translate laugh, scripts reply as you talk, 'Yes'
New Libertine gone Cult Head 'Clock of Sun!
I chose this and I chose this over you and you

Time-fuckers, Short hands throw long shapes
Your puppet strings. Damn my suction boots
Are choosing night and day there is no gravity.

Plan B

I was Heath Ledger playing Bob Dylan,
there was this roof-top scene, I paused. He said

*Once, maybe, you could sing
about Mary Hamilton and lemon trees,*

*But they took away the meaning, Alice.
I was a pawn in their game.*

You were Charlotte Gainsbourg in the film
standing by the mouth of playground slide.

We both said 'It's not about me anymore.'

I wore sunglasses. You caught my daughters.
I wrote a love song babe that calls you an idiot.

The Plan

*You shuffle, I look, split pack, you look back,
I shuffle, we deal same each, gamble, win all*

*summer, double or nothing, little flutter, rain,
thunder, freeze loan, delicate, fold, go again,*

*wait year, text joke (insert sparkle pony-up
long shot) marry in secret, no fuss, neither*

need ask, just fact: a Bee, a Bird, Japanese
honey-worm-noodles, jet chatter, air guitar

vintage chopper, sky, land, song bee buzzing?

Caroline Bird

TALKING ABOUT BOB DYLAN TO IWAN LLWYD

i.m. Iwan Llwyd, 1958-2010

Every gutter
a lagoon, and the Santa Ritas foaming
through the downpour on the way to the station,
bare-chested boys pretending
to surf along Olimpio.

Above us
on the corrugated roof
the thunder sounded like a rivet gun.
At the counter I went on talking,
but imagine by then you had heard enough.

Think of all
that woogie boogie, I said.
Another electric storm in another
auditorium, two more hours
so the bootleggers can compare set lists.

Seems to me,
you laughed, that misses the point.
What else is a man supposed to do?
Look, how he behaves now
makes it possible for the rest of us.

And whether
rio or riacho, the water
rolled in its red oils past the rodoviaria,
neither of us willing to be the first
to walk into the rain.

Robert Minhinnick

COMING BACK WITH JT
AND BOB DYLAN

*Returning to Wales on the train. They used to call it
the 125 but they don't do that now.*

There is downpour, always.
Fat rain hung over South Wales
like a diseased lung.
'There's many here among us
who think that life is but a joke.'
Dylan, walkman, bright chrome band
of earphones across my head
like a scar. Drove a shunter
once at Severn Tunnel. All the yards
now flat. Church with its spire,
stranger pointing a swollen finger.
Yellow rape bright in the rain,
land gouged by road and drain.

Tripp returning from foreign England
40 years back wanted border guards
to keep the place the same. But the terraces fail
and the tracks are crapped over with pitchmastic.
Jesus Saves – The Fuck He Does – white slapped
on a bridge side. Industry made hardcore
for car park. Half of Wales with a
chipboard wardrobe still overweight
still dying of wet heart attack.
'They stone you when you're fit and able'.
Two beers with JT's ghost in the swaying bar
full of men in bad suits who
sell and never go home.
Intellect and dignity buried.
The land leveed with golf, junk and garbage.
And God somewhere   making it worse.

Peter Finch

NO DIRECTION HOME

In memory of Gregory O'Donoghue

I wrote that the final days of August would find me
washed up, propped in a place where the light of day
is tight and mean. You approved, gently tending –
even laments for summer were safe with you,
lines too concerned with the small ambit of seasons
to encompass the impact of a true ending.

And so it was that August swept you off your feet,
quenched your breath with ease as she dragged
hurricanes and swollen waters in her train.
In the middle of your fifty-fourth year –
one of the bald facts mourners swapped at the grave,
suddenly aware that they did not know you.

I knew only the grace of your yellowed fingers,
that elegant pen, your hand feathering its tender script
across a page, your hooded eyes, your mug of gin,
the small room where we met once a week.
I saw you sometimes walking lopsidedly in the street;
once, at a launch, we talked about Bob Dylan

but in the moment I heard of your death I knew
that you had guided me to a place – a room, a page –
where limping and stammering come into their own,
a vast, airy space inviting me to stand my ground,
to bellow in tantrum, to rampage, to thrive
in my brokenness.

Mary Noonan

ON BLUE WATER AND
BIRD VIEW

where the sun sinks into the hold of the ocean
and a wild wind blows across Point Dume –

not that I know how they say the word here
but it's Doom in my book, today –

Doom where the light's almost lost in the rollers
and spray rises up
into pillars and plumes
and a shimmering wind-dog roams the Malibu hills.

Though it's best to say nothing
on nights like this – when everything's already going west.

Just walk the road past the upsinger's place,
beneath the swaying trees
where a horse and two mules graze
and the ambulance still waits.

If it's help you need he said
            then I guess you better take this....

That was years ago – it looks so rusty now,
parked behind the chain-link fence
out on the bluff where long-gone Indians sleep –

it's their song he sings in a voice like the wind,
on a night like this,
in the Fall,
when the ocean comes calling
and opens the ancient door.

Cliff Fell

SEEING BOB DYLAN
WITH MY FATHER

We take our seats in the Sheffield Arena.
I haven't seen you in over a year
but you still wear that permanent shrug
as if you couldn't have expected more
than your family, and a job packing bottles
that passes the days and pays the bills.

On rare days we had the house to ourselves
you'd slip LPs from the cupboard like secrets:
Highway 61 Revisited, The Freewheelin' Bob Dylan,
racing rhythms or a simple guitar and voice,
that lifted us beyond the redbrick terrace
to candlelit bedsits and winter alleys.

This skeletal steeltown became a smudge
on my horizon, but I came back to bring you
here. Dylan plays like a man starting over,
writing the songs all over again,
and the words we share along with him
take the place of things we'll never say.

Andrew Forster

MOST LIKELY YOU GO YOUR WAY AND I'LL GO MINE

1

Bob Dylan goes his way and perhaps purchases cigarettes
He wonders who if not himself could jump this gate
He wonders whose is the youngest soul in hell
He looks out for his reflection
but only to check his pencil-thin moustache
Any reflection will do
A puddle a shop window
The moustache on the girl playing hopscotch
the moustache on the dog
are looking fine
His moustache must be looking fine as well

2

Bob Dylan figures that his name may just as well
be replaced by any other
Roger Maris for example or Pierre Reverdy
Felix the Cat Tokyo Rose or Casanova
Another day has started and he places
a potted yellow flower on the window ledge
Somewhere between the grooves of a record
that is playing Bob Dylan thinks he foresees his death
Saint Thomas Stack-a-Lee Zarathustra
This is his death as revealed to him
a ray of emerald light from a sliver
of sky between two buildings
shatters his roadshow like roots through stone
But he figures that this death may just as well
be owned by any other
that it was perhaps
Phillipe Soupault's Le Corbusier's Evan Kennedy's

3

It occurs to Bob Dylan that his voice bears
many similarities to Edith Piaf's
at least enough urging him to comment
There is a switch in his head
as well as
in everyone else's and in the corner
of the room in which the switch is installed
is a bucket
and in the bucket a mop
La Vie en Rose L'Homme à la Moto
Someone please flip this switch s'il vous plait
The hands of Edith Piaf must have been softer
than Bob Dylan's but she never played guitar
only sang of one
And if it is the exact guitar now occupying
a corner of the room Bob Dylan occupies
we cannot be sure
There is no way of guessing
And whether its song is sweeter than what
can be strummed on the mop in that cozy room
in Bob Dylan's mind is in a way
a matter of taste

4

Bob Dylan pulls up a chair at the only bar
he has never been to

Its lamps please Bob Dylan's eyes
so much he is prepared to comment
until he realizes his thoughts of the lamps
in another bar
a bar he frequents quite a bit
are influencing his current impressions

So much for the lamps he thinks
The bartender mistakes Bob Dylan
for Reggie Jackson
greatest New York Yankee
ever to play right field

What's your poison Mr. October he says
though it is clear to the patrons of this bar
that this man is not Reggie Jackson
but rather Emma Goldman
greatest American anarchist
ever to play right field

Bob Dylan does not correct him
but instead asks for a bowl of grapes
to which the bartender replies
that this is not a fruit stand
but a bar and that no grapes can be sold

Thinking he was not understood
that perhaps the bartender is new
Bob Dylan requests a second time
the bowl of grapes
to which the bartender replies that if
there is a third request for the grapes
he will nail Bob Dylan's beak to the bar floor
and roast him
The bartender is clearly mistaking this patron
for a duck that waddled in

Bob Dylan waddles out of the bar
only to return the next night and request
from the bartender surely the same bartender
a bowl of grapes

Yankee or not
the bartender replies
this is not the establishment
to serve you a bowl of grapes

as he reaches into a dark cabinet
a cabinet good for storing a hammer and nails
to which Bob Dylan gets off the barstool
and leaves
not quite offended

5

At the drugstore Bob Dylan hears
playing through the entire store a song
he will not compose for another ten years
There is no mistaking his voice albeit aged
ten years but ten years of what
Bob Dylan asks aloud
We must ask this too
The voice sounds optimistic so it must be
a good ten years

But what of this refrain he asks
gesturing us over
and pointing to the round white speaker built into the
ceiling
this refrain about the moon falling apart

There is commotion in the next aisle
one Bob Dylan rarely browses
Two women argue over his relevance
and quote not only lines in this song
but others he has yet to write
songs Bob Dylan cannot wait to hear

Bob Dylan buys nothing
He is outside where night has fallen
It was day when he first walked in and now
there is the moon still in one piece

Bob Dylan will have to wait here
Bob Dylan wants to see it happen himself

Evan Kennedy

HANGMAN SONNET

Life together was still good but the first tiles
were slipping loose. They played Hangman
before the gig, swinging the names of songs
from the noose then peeling off round the back
till they reached a line of three black coaches
parked up in the loading area, band and crew,
they guessed, and the star's twisted eyrie.
There was no one about. They sparked up
a couple of bombers and kept look-out
before threading slowly through the disabled
parking bay to join the crowd in the main arena
and the folk remedy of the songs' interior,
the figure on the hangman's noose from
'All Along the Watchtower' – the Joker not the Thief.

Tim Cumming

PINNACLES

And as there is no chance of sleep
you'll spend the hours considering all the sounds
rain could be against the fabric of the tent:
the tuning of a radio, the static of a zillion midges,
hard applause, crumpled foil, the barking of a silver dog
who wants sometimes just to stop and not have to go on.

And you'll seek your own addition to the consensus
of the audible, until the river you're pitched by
comes to recognize your tread, the rhyming of your breath,
as you rest your ear to the ground
to track where the music's coming from,
wanting sometimes just to stop and not have to go on.

The worsening of the mountains confounds you.
They blacken, faceless, and you can't figure
how to look at them, or how to ignore them,
whether they are beautiful, or terrible, or if they could cure
you.
And so you lie there sighing like a slide guitar,
wanting sometimes just to stop, and not have to go on.

Rachael Boast

LIKE THE LIVING END

(an elegy for David Mather 1954-2010)

'Home is where one starts from ...
... old stones that cannot be deciphered.'
T.S. Eliot, 'East Coker'

'I stole away and cried.'
Bob Dylan

1

After all the journeying
suddenly you see it: our river
with its reaches in their estuary light,
the sandbank outlines at low tide
and streams flowing forward to Seaforth.

After all, the journeying
that took you from yourself forever
forever returns you, though not quite,
home being never the same –
but come here for a funeral
you have it, don't you, that bereavement
in every departure, like its foretaste,
and each return a fostering
of distances, the sun-glare
now it glints on far refineries
as we've rounded Weston Point.

Above the bridge, an easyJet
plane descends to the renamed airport,
and in its higher sky's
releases, burdens being lifted
from you into the uneventful air
were shaming re-stirred memories
of girls, Dave, drunken parties,
those all-night games of Hearts
while cars on Mather Avenue

or police dogs barking in their kennels
brought them back, and you
can start again from there.

2

This one's in a minor key,
its black notes to be borne in mind,
the accidentals, obbligatos,
all those terms I'd learned by heart –
con brio, lento, da capo al fine,
rallentando in the street,
unadopted, past St Catherine's,
with its cobblestones tumbling away
to raw earth and rubble.

Although you can't go any more,
are out of touch, I've come
back to a map of unvisitable places:
Darlington Street, for instance,
memorials which don't match the scene
where terraces' sandblasted
smuts become a pinkish red –
the post-Orwellian word-face
with its piss-pot, blocked waste-pipe,
flight of locks and pier,
its self-esteem in your capable hands…

That's where my music teacher's house was,
where I would go to play the pieces,
her black door like an omen;
scolded, told off for not practicing enough,
would repeat that performance week after week.
But this late morning, momentarily lost
and driven here by accident,
it was as if I'd been
trespassing yet again on my own past.

3

Then the bridge, the bridge was
like a major variation
taking us over railway lines
when summer itself had seemed to shudder;
dazzling with its last gasp,
it had knocked the stuffing out of
those loiterers behind a hearse
in unclouded sunshine.

Underneath the yew trees
acres of headstones were shining around us:
our eyes adjusted to that glare;
pasts were hovering in the shadows
down Cemetery Road, at Ince;
mourners caught up with each other,
and surely my dad had brought me here
when on funeral duty once.

So that now in its chapel of rest,
and shaking myself, I was like
some astonished archaeologist
who's just unearthed your grave-goods:
black vinyl discs, tapes, silver CDs,
headphones, and a new guitar,
East Coker's measured words –
distractions for an afterlife,
your music, your music wherever you are.

4

No, the dead can't live on bread alone:
I'm at it again, co-opting them
for my own purposes
as when, assuming there's no way back,
home literally never the same,
we did revisit it once, remember?

Remember us wandering in that churchyard,
its separate plots grid-referenced
as on a street map, numbered
and spelt out along the low walls?
Then the present incumbent accosted us:
trespassing, we were trespassing
on his pastures, in a word.

But, told, he graciously showed us round
that past: subsided church porch
where under our feet coal-seams had collapsed,
and his vicarage lacking some upstairs rooms
for, saving costs, they had altered its roofline,
demolishing the one
in which my sister was born, later mine –
a space of thin air;
there, I heard him on Radio Caroline.

5

Then I'd have to get out of the house again,
traverse old love's domain
across Mather, this Friday morning,
then Menlove Avenue, another pun there!
to Quarry Street and Newstead farm
built from warm sandstone cut out of its hill;
it brings home all our pining.

Treading down indecipherable stones
anew, like a revenant-returnee,
that vicar's son from *Cranford*,
I come back in the nick of time
to local librarians beginning their day
down shelves where love began
for you, Dave, making my drunken words
wrong as can be, after all our pining,
and sluggard children are taken to school
this September morning.

Though the past used to be another country
now a film truck's parked amid groves
by remnants of Allerton Towers
and, yes, our yesterdays, all of them,
turn into fiction, for grim
death would put an end to our loves.

6

The golf course in those grounds
of its tumble-down estate
has columns, plinths, an obelisk
in the local sandstone
seen taper into sky last spring;
yes, and like that time before
by way of convalescing,
I made a fairway tour.

Chestnut candles rose behind
laburnum tendrils, and
an aging intellect might turn
to the new wisteria,
but couldn't compete with them and their
natural recurrences –
surviving through broad daylight.

Uncanny in both senses,
life histories among neglect
at such dilapidations,
old stones that cannot be deciphered
have grown forgetful now,
as if those years had never happened …
oh and the crumbling relations
here, at an eighteenth hole,
are fallen blocks, tagged stones;
like it's the living end.

7

Still I see myself leaping from the wrong train,
guitar-case in hand,
as it headed not for Durham
but on towards a siding
that weekend, the first time we heard
his 'Simple Twist of Fate'
when I came to visit in Providence Row
so that girlfriend of mine could meet her other
lover, though he didn't show ...

One of your mourners had quoted the album,
you making us 'lonesome when you go'
and Hawys, your distraught widow,
clutching at her photographs
for love's not most nearly itself under starlight
or lamplight with a family album
(forgive me, forgive me I'm co-opting *you* now).

But what else can I do with our dead ones
as we become people from history too?
Glad to be of use, you're helpful still,
don't want to cause her pain,
practising duets with me
like this one in a minor key
with black notes to be borne in mind?
Let's try it one more time again.

Peter Robinson

NOTE
The epigraph from T.S. Eliot's 'East Coker', the second of *Four Quartets*,
cites two phrases from the final passage in the poem, which was read as
part of David Mather's funeral service at Wigan Crematorium, Ince, on 2
September 2010. Bob Dylan's early song 'He was a Friend of Mine' was
also played in tribute to his lifelong obsession with the singer's entire
output, an obsession I share.

CHANGED MY WAY OF THINKING

Time past, I thought that love was just
a lazy sprawl across a big brass bed.
Yes, I know there was more to what you said,
but I didn't really listen to the rest.

Those were the days of the Rendezvous Cafe,
laughing as we gossiped and ignored the clock
in a room made of music, your songs on the juke box
chiming their sorcery into each new Saturday.

Time past, I thought the world would change,
your fist of truth punch holes of jagged shame
through every dirty window, each sinner named
one less obstacle in a system we would rearrange.

Those were the days I sneered at rules and straight,
unquestioning girls and blokes,
who didn't seem to know the Bomb would turn us all to smoke,
or didn't care enough for peace to demonstrate.

Since, I've spun senseless, drunk on dreams and wine.
I've known desire and worn a ring
that sparkles and a ring that lost its shine.
I've been where loss has broken everything.

Since, I've asked, *What good am I?* Served
causes, men and children, then I've served myself.
I've seen the changing of the guard, power preserved
by pin-men low on principle and high on wealth.

The world's gone wrong. I've seen the waters rise.
Even the answer from the wind is, *It's not me.*
No mercy now, we're out of time and out of alibis.
If anything's beyond all this, it's still a mystery.

The Rendezvous Cafe was flattened long ago –
but you keep on. And I'm still hanging on your songs,
still working out the deal that legislates what train we're on.
No golden bed exists. Never give up loving though.

Chrissy Banks

IF YOUR PARENTS LIKE DYLAN IT MEANS THEY WERE COOL

My mum liked The Beatles, she knitted coat-hanger covers
with 'The Beatles' set into geometric patterns of sky
and navy wool. She must have worked it out on graph paper.

I found them at fourteen and hope she hasn't thrown them
out –
they are a testament to a young life in Nottinghamshire,
my dad would have been getting into Sci-Fi.

My partner's parents own the whole of Dylan.
His dad hitchhiked almost to Woodstock then,
with five miles to go, stopped for a week to get high.

After six years together our parents still haven't met.
The Atlantic helps, although they have exchanged gifts:
a calendar of Inuit Art for one of English Wildlife.

Holly Hopkins

EVERYWHERE'S NOWHERE

Bob Dylan at 70

The years accumulate as left behinds,
like city signposting viewed from a car,
the outlet malls, rainy red LED displays,
one gig replaced by another's
whiteout amnesia, the moon-faced white
polymer coating on a sleeping pill,

it goes that way, a lost moment's
one hundred years ago, it's Tallahassee,
Alabama, New York, London O2,
always the full-on explosive present
littering like a contrail – shotgun songs
shattered with vocal bullet-holes,

the scorch-marks burning fingers, snapping strings,
the road extends his life five thousands times,
his air-miles shimmy in global carbon,
the body narrated into the pull
of lyric gravity – you hear it too
an edgy spiked-up 'Like a Rolling Stone'

or desperate 'Tangled Up In Blue',
the songs familiar now as oxygen;
the car burns on through foggy Birmingham,
Nashville – a biker on the road
doing a crazy segue – and he's gone
sloganing CB&B – Bush & Blair

Criminal Blood Brothers, a red sun up,
an uncapped bottle of Jack Daniels
targeting raw spots – there's so much to learn
from whiskey's altered state intelligence
under a raw jet-rumbling urban dawn
like a popped tomato, moving on again

into the hills – and it's a Dylan day,
the exchange of place central to the art
of moving songs round like playing mah-jong,
blues at their heart, lifted out of the land
as tribal rhythm – and he picks it up,
the pieces quickly filled in by the band.

Jeremy Reed

SEVENTY CAKES AROUND
A CANDLE

Ran away to join the carnie, skipped
grade school, scrambled the gutter
before the sun poured down its drain,
up and over the slag heaps – the town
that moved – hop scotching the sleepers
when no hum was on the line, blue eyes
bright with lights like stars; how they
twinkled that night the dark got inside.

Never the same again – Jim Crack Corn,
black faced master of the boater and cane,
tapped out a tune, then sang it loud and pure,
his mouth a tunnel bands marched through,
gospel choirs swayed inside, hobos jumped
box cars for; a medicine show, the dealer of cures.

> *Ten cakes around a candle,*
> *Ten candles round a cake.*

Scrawny as a Pinscher's favourite bone
Bobby gives Manhattan the finger,
sticks his thumb towards Minnesota
with the best cherry pie in Hibbing
eating up his mind. Damn fine to be
on the road again, teen years done
as the Iron Range splits down the seam
and the Great Lakes crack up laughing.

Man, no one says 'man' anymore
but they did then: man-hugs in the porch,
they called him a man as the sweep
of his family brushed the dust of snow
through that crack below the door,
the north country drifting inside him.

> *Twenty cakes around a candle,*
> *Twenty candles round a cake.*

Said too much, doesn't have much to say.
He'd give up a decade to have a decade back.
Before the crash, he was crashing every day
and now life's slow, and he likes that.
New York just isn't New York anymore,
the country has gone country or to pot
and Weberman's on the phone or at the door;
if something doesn't start, this has to stop.

Bob's head to rock at the Wailing Wall
with ten plagues of Egypt gnawing at his cheek,
petitioning whosoever with a prayer.
The chosen of the chosen. It takes Jewish balls
to sit at the feet of those whose feet
the Lord sat at, back then – somewhere over there.

> *Thirty cakes around a candle,*
> *Thirty candles round a cake.*

A pirate looks forty in the eye.
An eye that wears a patch. And that patch
is painted with an eye. And that eye
looks back, dead as a sharp shooter
who's been sniped. Forty is the barrel
of a gun only the lucky look down,
and if the good half of life is now done
then there's a lesser half still to go.

And if the first half meant hard travelling
the second is spent all at sea
with home no particular direction
and what treasure he had, buried in his sleep
down a hole on some forgotten island.
X marks the spot. Dig hard. Dig deep.

> *Forty cakes around a candle,*
> *Forty candles round a cake.*

Is this what they call never ending?
When you call on Dave, and Dave's wife
lets you in, sits you down, phones Dave
to let him know you're there. Dave says
'Who is this guy?' and she says 'He looks
like the man in the band with the woman
who looks like a man.' 'Oh, him,' Dave says.
You make your excuses, get out of Dave's house.

Cross that bridge you crossed in your top hat
and coat, sit down in that same seat, now
wearing a cap and two hoods, order a shot,
sit down to sketch out the waitress
or the window, whichever seems closer
when the light falls onto the page.

> *Fifty cakes around a candle,*
> *Fifty candles round a cake.*

Some say it's post-modern to steal
so let's steal whatever comes to hand.
Why do words, once in order, become owned?
Ask the Yakuza – writing a song
is like losing a bone, only so many
before a man falls down. Dylan
in the corner with his cut-ups and glue,
the judge, the jury, prosecutor and accused...

Exhibit one – something old. Exhibit two –
something new. And this little something
was borrowed from the blues. As if
the Mississippi never flowed to the sea,
and fell as hail on Lake Superior, where
a boy went fishing once, and never came back.

> *Sixty cakes around a candle,*
> *Sixty candles round a cake.*

Let's play fantasy dinner parties.
Sat in his head, that man in the hat.
More empty chairs than he can deal with –
missing Nelson, Lefty, Elvis and Frank,
while Woody still shakes up his bed.
So fill your boots with the bass man's gumbo
and feed the Doberman knuckle bones,
watch him suck them dry of marrow,

Take pleasure in what no one says, or knows.
Under the great dome of Malibu
or on the ranch, where the sky is big
as the America this man swallowed whole
and made it bigger, and will live to see
it shrink when the party has to end...

> *Seventy cakes around a candle,*
> *Seventy candles round a cake.*

Damian Furniss

HOW LIKE

And I am wondering about your face,
how it alters when a mood takes hold.

Such a changeling
        like a sparrow, like a burning flutter,
        higher and higher up into the tree.

Like a breath by cold night,
the crispest revelation breaking ice.
What is left is the warmest sensation at the pit of stomach.

How like a stretched metaphor you are,
        how like broken branches from an apple tree.
        Like its fallen fruit half-eaten by animals.

How like a mystery,
entangled by the twang of a country that can't own you.
How like an endless path of thought.

How like a mesmeriser
        with the power of foresight.
        How like his instruments buzzing blackly across my mind.

How like the concept of the wheel,
of the science of silence.
How like etcetera in the tall, green grasses.

How like a slipperiness of truth slithering by and by.
        How like the moon in all of its tiredness,
        of the river who waits for the clearest direction to your door.

Libby Hart

HIS

I only ask this now now silence asks it
Of me only.
Asks it of the last man in the world
Expecting it and if I were that man
And / or that lonely

Yes I might expect it. When I topple
Back from this
White screen I must admit there's really no one.
I only ask this now now silence asks me
This: what if His –

You clock that H and scarper, it can not
Be run from.
You're looking at it now and now whatever
Thing you are you're running home to where
You come from –

What if His – what if his – what if his
Question
As to why – why have you – why have You –
Gone? was the only time he ever mentioned
Anyone

He thought was there? Then he toppled back away
Into the care
Of nothing that would last and while it lasted
All he did was build what would be there
Were He there.

Glyn Maxwell

ACKNOWLEDGEMENTS

'Killing Time #2' by Simon Armitage is from *Travelling Songs* (Faber, 2004)

'Pinnacles' by Rachael Boast is to be published in *Sidereal* (Picador, 2011)

'Plutarch' by Matthew Caley is from *Dancing in the Lone-Star Diner* (Slow Dancer, 1988), and 'Acquiesence' is from *Apparently* (Bloodaxe, 2010)

'Tangled Up in Blue' by Glenn Cooper is from *Tryin' to Get to Heaven* (Blind Dog Press, 2009)

'40th Birthday with Cassette Deck and Questions' by Tim Dooley is from *Imagined Rooms* (Salt, 2010)

'On Blue Water and Bird View' by Cliff Fell was first published in an earlier version in *Beauty of the Badlands* (Victoria University Press, 2008)

'Jack of Hearts' by Lawrence Ferlinghetti is from *Who Are We Now?*, copyright Lawrence Ferlinghetti, 1976. Reprinted by permission of New Directions Publishing Corporation.

'Coming Back with JT and Bob Dylan' by Peter Finch is from *Zen Cymru* (Seren, 2010)

'The Nightingale's Code' by Mark Ford is from *Soft Sift* (Faber, 2001)

'Blue Gossip' by Allen Ginsberg first appeared in *First Blues: Rags, Ballads and Harmonium Songs, 1971-1974* (Full Court Press, New York, 1975)

'How Like' by Libby Hart first appeared in *Eureka Street Magazine* (Australia)

'The Voice' by Paul Henry is from *The Brittle Sea: New and Selected Poems* (Seren, 2010)

'Hard Rain' by Tony Hoagland is from *Unincorporated Persons in the Honda Dynasty* (Bloodaxe, 2010)

'The Last Waltz' by Douglas Houston is from *With the Offal Eaters* (Bloodaxe, 1986)

'Song for Bob Dylan' by Norbert Krapf is from *The Country I Come From* (Archer Books, 2002)

'Eidolon' by Roddy Lumsden first appeared in *Poetry Magazine* (May 2010)

'Minnesota Harmonica Man' by Lachlan Mackinnon is from *The Jupiter Collisions* (Faber, 2003)

'Younger Than That Now' by Glyn Maxwell is from *Rest for the Wicked* (Bloodaxe, 1995)

'Ode' by Michael McClure is from *Jaguar Skies* (New Directions, 1975)

'Bob Dylan and the Blue Angel' by Roger McGough is from *Everyday clipses* (Penguin/Viking, 2002) reprinted by kind permission of Charles Walker Associates.

'Bob Dylan at Princeton, November 2000' by Paul Muldoon is from *Horse Latitudes* (Faber, 2006)

'Shooting Star' by Robert Polito is from *Hollywood & God* (University of Chicago Press, 2009)

'Before the Roadshow' by Patricia Pogson is from *Before the Roadshow* (Rivelin Press)

'Like the Living End' by Peter Robinson has been accepted for publication in *Envoi*

'Digesting Crab Claws' and 'Postcard of a Hanging' by Matthew Sweeney are from *Blue Shoes* (Secker & Warburg, 1989)

'Legacy' by Susan Utting is from *Houses Without Walls* (Two Rivers Press, 2007)

'Aisle Sixteen Revisited' by Luke Wright is from *High Performances* (Nasty Little Press, 2009)

CONTRIBUTORS' NOTES

ANON after HAFEZ. Hafez (1320-1388) is the great lyric poet of Iran, famous for his ghazals that traditionally deal with love and wine, ecstasy and freedom from restraint.

SIMON ARMITAGE is a freelance writer, broadcaster and playwright who has written extensively for radio and televison. His translation of *Sir Gawain and the Green Knight* was published in 2007, his most recent collection was *Seeing Stars* (Faber 2010).

CHRISSY BANKS recalls first hearing Dylan on the jukebox of The Rendezvous Cafe on the Isle of Man. Her favourite song of his is 'Love Minus Zero/No Limit', her most recent collection *Days of Fire and Flood* (Original Plus, 2004).

RACHELLE BIJOU is a widely published New York poet who now lives in Paris. She was the recipient of the 2009 Norman Mailer Writer's Award.

CAROLINE BIRD was born in 1986. Her first collection *Looking Through Letterboxes* was published by Carcanet in 2002, her most recent is *The Watering Can* (Carcanet, 2009). She came to both poetry and Dylan after a reading of Phil Bowen's *Jewels and Binoculars* at the West Yorkshire Playhouse in 1994 when still a little girl.

NATHANIEL BLUE lived in New York during the 1960s and L.A. in the seventies, where he worshipped at the Hollywood Vineyard Church as did Bob Dylan. He is now a Pentecostalist missionary based in Darjeeling. His only poetry collection was *Showboat Joe* (Boxcar Press, 1969).

RACHAEL BOAST at an early age recognised Bob Dylan as someone who did what his artistic conscience told him: go the extra mile, tap the source, honour and perpetuate it. *Sidereal* will be published by Picador in 2011.

PHIL BOWEN first heard Bob Dylan on Radio Luxemburg in 1964. He was amazed to find out how young he was with a voice like that. Recent publications include: *Nowhere's Far – New & Selected Poems 1990-2008* (2009) and *Cuckoo Rock* (2010) both with Salt Publications.

MATT BRYDEN was most affected by Dylan when a friend bought *Blonde on Blonde* on the strength of the cover. By the beginning of 'Pledging My Time', all the Doors cassettes bought earlier were redundant. His first collection *Night Porter* (2010) won the Templar Poetry Competition.

MATHEW CALEY wrote 'Plutarch' after recalling an interview Dylan gave talking about the 13th century poet mentioned in 'Tangled Up In Blue'. His most recent collection is *Apparently* (2010, Bloodaxe). 'Aquiescence' from that book is very loosely-based on the Dylan song 'Isis' from *Desire*.

PETER CARPENTER is the current Chair of the Poetry Society. He has published five collections; his *New and Selected Poems* is published by Smith/Doorstop in 2012. His favourite concert was one at Earl's Court in 1978; his favourite cover version is Steve Knightly's 'Senor'.

LINDA CHASE is from New York, lives in Manchester and is director of Poets and Players, a poetry and music series. Her third Carcanet book, *Not Many Love Poems*, will be published in 2011. Bob is two months older than Linda and she says that's why he has more wrinkles.

SUZANNE CONWAY completed an MA in Creative Writing at Sussex University and won the Asham Award for Poetry in 1998. She is published widely in magazines and is completing her first collection. Her most memorable Dylan moment is in her poem 'Don't Think Twice'.

GLENN COOPER feels Bob Dylan has most deeply touched his life by opening his mind to other singers, writers, painters and thinkers, and feels all roads ultimately lead to him. His collection *Tryin To Get To Heaven*, (Blind Dog Press, 2009) deals exclusively with this theme.

TIM CUMMING writes about music and the arts for the British and international press. He has never interviewed Bob Dylan but did once discuss music and sauces with Bruce Langhorne, the Tambourine Man. His poetry was featured in Bloodaxe's recent anthology *Identity Parade.*

ANDY DARLINGTON is a Yorkshire based poet and music journalist currently reviewing DVDs for the Videovista website, writing about Folk & Roots music for *R2: Rock 'n' Reel* magazine. His favourite Dylan song is still 'Just Like Tom Thumb's Blues' but 'Not Dark Yet' is running it close.

MATTHEW DICKMAN was born in Oregon in 1975. He has been published in *The New Yorker* and his first book *The All-American Poem* (Copper Canyon Press) was the winner of the 2008 American Poetry Review's First Book Prize in Poetry.

TIM DOOLEY has published two collections: *Keeping Time* (Salt, 2008) and *Imagined Rooms* (Salt, 2010). *Another Side of Bob Dylan* was his first record after seeing the BBC specials in 1965. The first time he saw him play was at the Isle of Wight in 1969 when Dylan wore a white suit.

JANE DRAYCOTT is a PBS Next Generation poet. Her collections include: *Over* (TS Eliot Prize shortlist 2009) and *Prince Rupert's Drop* (Forward shortlist 1999). Her first Dylan seed was the green and flame-snakes of hair poster - and nothing to do with the folk club where she bought it.

CLIFF FELL has had two collections published by Victoria University Press: *The Adulterer's Bible* (2003) – shortlisted for the New Zealand Book Awards – and *Beauty of the Badlands* (2008). 'Blue Water and Bird View' refers to streets which run alongside Dylan's estate in Malibu.

LAWRENCE FERLINGHETTI (born 1919) co-founded City Light Books in San Francisco in 1953. His *Coney Island of the Mind* has over one million copies in print. He is one of the poets (with Michael McClure) featured in Martin Scorsese's 1978 film about The Band, *The Last Waltz*.

PETER FINCH is a poet and critic based in Cardiff. He is Chief Executive of Literature Wales. He works in both traditional and experimental forms and is best known for his declamatory and highly original poetry readings.

MARK FORD is Professor of English at University College London. He completed a doctorate at Oxford on the poetry of John Ashbery, and is a regular contributor to the *New York Review of Books*. His most recent collection is *Soft Sift* (Faber, 2003).

ANDREW FORSTER is Literature Officer for the Wordsworth Trust at Dove Cottage in Grasmere. His collection *Fear of Thunder* (Flambard Press) was shortlisted for the Forward Prize for Best First Collection in 2008. His poem realises how deeply Dylan's music has touched his life.

LINDA FRANCE remembers listening to *Desire* as a student in the seventies. She's warmed more and more to Dylan as they've both got older and mellower. In 1993 she edited the much acclaimed *Sixty Women Poets* (Bloodaxe). Her most recent collection is *You Are Her* (Arc, 2010).

DAMIAN FURNISS first heard Bob Dylan on an Open University radio documentary about the civil rights movement when he was thirteen, tuning in from under the bedclothes when he should have been listening to John Peel. His first full collection is *Chocolate Che* (Shearsman, 2010).

JOHN GIBBENS is a poet, musician and journalist. He is the author of *The Nightingale's Code – A Poetic Study of Bob Dylan* (Touched Press, 2001) His earliest recollection of Dylan is listening to *Bringing It All Back Home* as an eight year old. His favourite song is 'Brownsville Girl'.

ALLEN GINSBERG published *Howl* in 1956 making him the foremost American poet of the Beat Generation. He first met Bob Dylan in New York at the end of 1963 and remained a constant figure in Dylan's life – touring with him on the Rolling Thunder Revue – until his death in 1997.

ANN GRAY dedicated her last collection *At the Gate* (Headland, 2008) to Alan Sizer, who gave her 'You're Gonna Make Me Lonesome When You Go' for the journey home. Favourite Dylan songs include 'Clothes Line Saga' (by the Roche Sisters) and 'Lily, Rosemary and the Jack of Hearts'.

JOHN GOODBY is a poet, critic, and lecturer at Swansea University. His *Work of Words: Re-reading Dylan Thomas* is due from Liverpool University Press in 2012. A new poetry collection *The True Prize* is due from Cinnamon Press later this year. He favours the acoustic 'Visions of Johanna' from *Biograph* or the lushly sinister 'Senor' on *Street Legal*.

JUSTIN HAMM lives in Missouri. He is the author of *Illinois, My Apologies* (RockSaw Press, 2011). His work has appeared in *The New York Quarterly*, *The Brooklyn Review* and *Cold Mountain Review*.

LIBBY HART was born in Melbourne in 1971. Her first collection *Fresh News From the Arctic* (2006) won the Anne Elder Award. Her most recent collection is *This Floating World*, (Five Islands Press, 2011). Her favourite Dylan song is 'Not Dark Yet'.

GEOFF HATTERSLEY published *Back of Beyond – New & Selected Poems* (Smith/Doorstep) in 2006. He hosts monthly readings at The Albert in Huddersfield and has performed voice/guitar collaborations with Michael Massey at the Marsden International Jazz Festival.

PAUL HENRY is one of Wales's leading poets. He came to poetry through songwriting and to songwriting through Bob Dylan. *The Brittle Sea: New & Selected Poems* was published by Seren in 2010.

TONY HOAGLAND considers himself equidistant between Sharon Olds and Frank O'Hara on the aesthetic graph. His last collection was *Unincorporated Persons in the Late Honda Dynasty* (Bloodaxe, 2010). Awards include the Mark Twain Award from the Poetry Foundation in 2005.

HOLLY HOPKINS is formerly a Foyle's Young Poet of the Year and has poems in *Poetry Review*, *The Rialto* and in the anthologies *Bird Book* and *Coin Opera 2* (both Sidekick Press). She was introduced to Dylan by a teacher who set lyrics for the class to analyse instead of poems.

DOUGLAS HOUSTON was born in Cardiff in 1947, and grew up in Glasgow and London. His most recent collection is *Beyond the Playing Fields: New and Selected Poems 1980-2010*. He has admired Dylan's work since the mid-sixties for its lyrical, satirical, and political power.

PAMELA JOHNSON has published two novels: *Under Construction* and *Deep Blue Silence* (Sceptre); her third, *Taking In Water*, receiving an Arts Council Writers' Award. She teaches creative writing at Goldsmiths and has long relished Dylan's straight-talking, humour, cynicism and surrealism.

TERRY KELLY writes for the Bob Dylan magazine, *The Bridge*, having interviewed such luminaries as Christopher Ricks and Michael Gray. Dylan first entered his life in 1972, having borrowed *Bringing It All Back Home*. He favours *John Wesley Harding* of all Dylan albums.

EVAN KENNEDY is a poet from San Francisco who has written several chapbooks and a full-length collection, *Shoo-Ins to Ruin*, to be published in 2011 by Gold Wake.

ANGELA KIRBY was born in Lancashire in 1932 and lives in London. She was the BBC's Wildlife Poet of the Year in 1996 and in 2001. Her collections are: *Mr. Irresistible* and *Dirty Work* (Shoestring Press). A long-time

Dylan fan, *Blood on the Tracks* remains her favourite album.

NORBERT KRAPF admires the way Bob Dylan defies the expectations of his fans. As Poet Laureate of Indiana, he participated in seven performances of the Hoosier Dylan show. His ninth full-length collection, *Songs in Sepia and Black and White,* is forthcoming and will include fifteen poems about Bob Dylan.

PIPPA LITTLE was the recipient of an Eric Gregory Award. Her collection, *The Spar Box* (Vane Women) was a Poetry Book Society Choice. *Overwintering* comes out from Oxford Poets in 2012. She came to Dylan when music – particularly 'Visions of Johanna' – was something to help see her through.

RODDY LUMSDEN is a tutor for the Poetry School in London and is Commissioning Editor for Salt Publishing. *Mischief Night – New & Selected Poems* is published by Bloodaxe, as is *Identity Parade,* (2010, Editor). His favourite Dylan track is 'Caribbean Wind'. Favourite album, *Street Legal*.

MICHAEL McCLURE (born 1932) was one of the five poets (with Allen Ginsberg) who read at the legendary Six Gallery reading in San Francisco in 1956. He is famously photographed with Dylan and Ginsberg in Adler Alley at the group meeting of poets outside City Lights in December 5 1965.

ROGER McGOUGH, a Freeman of the City of Liverpool in 2001, met Bob Dylan there at the Blue Angel in 1965. His most recent collection is *That Awkward Age* (Penguin, 2009).

EDWARD MACKAY was born in the year of *Infidels*. He has been published in *London Grip, Sidekick Books* and *Clinic*. He has been shortlisted for an Eric Gregory Award and the Picador Poetry Prize. He lives in London and his favourite Dylan record is *Time Out of Mind*.

LACHLAN MACKINNON is a poet, critic and literary journalist. He was born in Aberdeen and educated at Charterhouse and Oxford. In 2010 he published *Small Hours* with Faber.

MARY MAHER is a widely published poet and painter who lives in Devon. Her much acclaimed first collection *Snowfruit* was selected for the first *Forward Anthology* in 1993. Her favourite Bob Dylan song is probably 'What Was It You Wanted' from *Oh Mercy*. Her novel *Relating to Michael* is due this year.

GLYN MAXWELL has won several awards for his poetry including the Somerset Maugham Prize and the Geoffrey Faber Memorial Prize. His play *The Lifeblood* won British Theatre Guide's 'Best Play' Award in 2004. His most recent collection is *Hide Now* (Picador, 2008).

CHRIS McCABE was born in Liverpool in 1977. Of his first collection, *The Hutton Inquiry* (Salt, 2005), the *Guardian* said "the whole book zooms by sparking with spot-on phrases". He currently works as the Joint Librarian at the Poetry Library in London

ROBERT MINHINNICK edited *Poetry Wales* from 1997-2008 and has twice won the Forward Prize for best poem. His novel *Sea Holly* (Seren, 2008) was shortlisted for the Ondaatje Prize. His poem here deals with a conversation with his late friend Iwan Llwyd in 2007.

PAUL MULDOON was born in County Tyrone and read English at Queens in Belfast. In 1987 he moved to the U.S.A. where he now teaches at Princeton. Awards include the T.S. Eliot Prize (1994) and the Pulitzer Prize (2003). Recent collections with Faber are *Plan B* (2009) and *Maggot* (2010).

MARY NOONAN has been published in many magazines including *The Cork Literary Review*. In 2009 she read at the Poetry Hearings festival in Berlin, and in 2010 was awarded the Listowel Poetry Collection Prize. Of Dylan albums, she loves the frontier melancholy of *Desire*.

PATRICIA POGSON was born in Fife and educated at Art Colleges in Preston and Oxford. In 1977 she married the poet Geoffrey Holloway – *Holding* (Flambard Press 2003) tells of their time together. She liked Dylan's film *Renaldo and Clara*, 'To Ramona' being a special song for her.

ROBERT POLITO directs the Graduate Writing Program at the New School in New York. His most recent collection is *Hollywood & God* (Chicago: University of Chicago Press, 2009).

JEREMY REED is Britain's foremost glamour poet, called 'a legend' by Pete Doherty. He has published 40 books of poetry, his most recent being *Piccadilly Bongo* (Enitharmon Press, 2010) with songs on CD by Marc Almond. He rates *Blood On The Tracks* and its outtakes as seminal genius.

PETER ROBINSON is Professor of English and American Literature at Reading University. His publications include: *Selected Poems* (Carcanet, 2003) and *The Look of Goodbye* (Shearsman, 2008). He's been listening to Dylan since *John Wesley Harding* and first saw him at the Isle of Wight in 1969.

PADRAIG ROONEY once owned a harmonica rack. His first collection *In The Bonsai Garden* won the Patrick Kavanagh Award in 1986. *The Fever Wards* was published by Salt in 2010. He first heard *Blonde on Blonde* in St. Macartan's College, Monaghan and lives in Basel Switzerland.

CAROL RUMENS writes a regular poetry blog for *Guardian* Books Online. Her most recent collection is *De Chirico's Threads* (Seren, 2010). Dylan is the singer who means the most, since hearing 'The Times They are A-Changin' sung badly at a London folk-club in the early sixties.

MATTHEW SWEENEY was short-listed for the T.S. Eliot award for *Black Moon* (Cape, 2007). His most recent collection is *The Night Post* (Salt,

2010). He was first drawn to Dylan in 1971, listening to 'Mr Tambourine Man' half a mile from the sea in his native Donegal. He now lives in Cork.

CHRISTOPHER TWIGG recalls Christopher Ricks saying that the only person who can never go to a Bob Dylan concert is Bob Dylan and he's also the only person who has to be at every concert. He has published two poetry collections *In the Choir* (Alces Press 1997) and *A Cherub That Sees Them* (Zenane 2003).

SUSAN UTTING first heard Dylan at the Albert Hall in 1965, the year before 'Judas!'. She had heard the records, but here was the man, making the words 'fit and mean', making them electric. Her latest collection is *Houses Without Walls* (Two Rivers Press).

PAUL VIOLI lives in New York and teaches at Columbia University. He is a recipient of the John Ciardi Lifetime Achievement Award. His most recent collection is *Overnight* (Hanging Loose, 2007).

GORDON WARDMAN is probably the only living writer to have been portayed on a trade union banner. His favourite Dylan album is *Nashville Skyline*.

ANTHONY WATTS is a Somerset poet who uniquely recalls the ill-fated 1962 TV play by Evan Jones, *Madhouse on Castle Street,* in which Dylan – on his first visit to London – played 'Bobby the Hobo' – and featured the first recorded version of 'Blowin' in the Wind' playing over the credits.

MILES WILDER in his lifelong quest for eloquence feels that Bob Dylan runs P.G. Wodehouse a close second. His verse play *Decadent in Dieppe* remains one of 'the great unfinisheds', but his *Getting it Right Guide* (co-edited with Sigmund Slingsby) will be available relatively soon.

DAVID WOOLLEY no longer works in Swansea. His latest collection is *Pursued by a Bear* (Headland, 2010). His favourite Bob Dylan song is no longer 'Lay Lady Lay'.

LUKE WRIGHT started performing poetry aged seventeen after seeing John Cooper Clarke, and in 2000 co-founded 'Aisle 16'. He devised *Powerpoint* for the Edinburgh Festival in 2004 and contributes to Radio 4's *Saturday Live*. Nasty Little Press published *High Performance* in 2009.

TAMAR YOSELOFF is the author of *Marks* with artist Linda Karshan (Pratt Contemporary Art, 2007) and editor of *A Room to Live In: A Kettle's Yard Anthology* (Salt, 2007). Her fourth collection *The City with Horns* is published by Salt in 2011. Her favourite Dylan album is *Blonde on Blonde*.